Mastering Market Trends

A Field Guide to Understanding and Interpreting Real Estate Data

Mastering Market Trends

A Field Guide to Understanding and Interpreting Real Estate Data

Cooper Thayer

Mastering Market Trends:
A Field Guide to Understanding and Interpreting Real Estate Data

Published by First&Lewis, an independent publishing imprint.
4833 Front Street, Unit B282
Castle Rock, CO 80104.

First edition
First printing

This book is provided for educational and informational purposes only. It is not legal, financial, tax, lending, appraisal, investment, brokerage compliance, accounting, or professional advice. Real estate laws, brokerage rules, market data sources, lending standards, financing conditions, appraisal practices, investor assumptions, and local market conditions vary by jurisdiction and change over time.

Readers should use professional judgment and consult appropriate licensed professionals when applying these concepts to specific transactions, client recommendations, investment decisions, or business practices. Examples, calculations, scenarios, and market interpretations in this book are intended to illustrate analytical concepts, not to prescribe a universal course of action.

Any references to real estate data, market reports, listing behavior, financing conditions, brokerage practice, or professional decision-making are used for explanatory purposes. Unless otherwise noted, examples are generalized or hypothetical and should not be read as representing a specific property, client, brokerage, MLS, lender, market, or transaction.

Third-party names, trademarks, service marks, trade names, association names, MLS names, platform names, and organization names are used for identification and explanatory purposes only. Their use does not imply endorsement, sponsorship, affiliation, or approval.

ISBN paperback: 979-8-234-14550-5
Library of Congress Control Number: 2026918197

Version Control Number: 1-072326-PUB

10 9 8 7 6 5 4 3 2 1

Contents

Market Data Is Not Market Understanding 9

Why Market Literacy Matters 13

The Market Is Not One Number 19

Median, Mean, and the Problem of Averages 25

The Cyclical Nature of Price 33

Interpreting Price Changes 39

Seasonality, Trendlines, and Headlines 47

The Pricing Path: Original List Price, Current List Price, and Close Price 55

Days on Market and Market Psychology 65

Price Reductions and Market Feedback 75

Price Per Square Foot and Its Problems 85

Inventory and Market Velocity 93

Supply, Demand, and Housing Market Mechanics 103

Months' Supply, Absorption Rate, and Market Balance 115

Mortgage Rates and Affordability 123

The Fed and the Housing Market 133

New Construction Signals 143

Residential Investment Metrics 151

How to Build a Market Read 161

How to Explain the Market to Clients 171

The Market Literacy Advantage 181

Better Interpretation, Better Decisions 187

About the Author 192

INTRODUCTION

Market Data Is Not Market Understanding

Real estate has largely solved the problem of getting numbers in front of people. Agents and clients now move through dashboards, MLS exports, market summaries, portal statistics, lender updates, headlines, newsletters, and social feeds that turn housing into a steady stream of reported facts, so the difficulty is rarely access to the number itself. It is what happens after the number appears.

A median sale price change can be accurate and still mislead the seller using it. Inventory can rise while buyers still feel like they have poor options. A headline about mortgage rates can be correct and still fail to explain what happens to payment, leverage, or timing once a real decision has to be made. A market report can be full of usable signals and still leave the actual question unanswered. Several things may be true at once and none of them, on its own, tells a seller where to price, a buyer how hard to push, or an agent which figure belongs in the conversation.

The numbers have to be sorted, framed, and interpreted before they become judgment instead of noise. This book is about that gap between reported data and usable judgment. Market literacy is the ability to understand what a number actually measures, what it leaves out, what comparison produced it, and whether it deserves to shape a real decision.

The Number and What It Means

The difference comes into focus in one very common mistake.

A seller reads that median sale prices in her metro area are up 11 percent year over year, and from that point forward the problem is not the absence of data but the meaning attached to it. She has a real number in front of her, but not yet an understanding of what that number actually describes. The median tells her where the middle of all the closed sales landed across a broad geography, all price ranges, all property types, and all conditions. It does not describe her home. It does not describe her neighborhood. It does not describe what a buyer will pay for her specific property, in its specific condition, competing against whatever else is currently listed.

When she applies the 11 percent to her home, she is not misreading the statistic so much as drawing from it an inference that feels reasonable and is wrong more often than it is right. The market went up, so her house went up the same amount. The logic may feel intuitive, but the conclusion is not reliable.

The agent who understands what the median actually measures can explain this without dismissing her expectation or arguing with the data. The point is not to tell the seller the number is wrong. The point is to show her what kind of answer the number can and cannot provide.

That is what often happens when a seller brings in a market summary and treats it like a pricing model. The report may say prices are up across the metro, and the seller may hear, *"My house should be up by that amount."* But the pricing question is narrower than the headline. It depends on the home's condition, the active competition, the price tier, the recent comparable sales, and what buyers in that segment are doing now. The market summary can be useful context, but it is not the full answer. The critical work is translating the broad number into the specific decision.

What Market Literacy Is

Market literacy is not economics or data science, and it requires no background beyond the ability to read a market report and ask what it *actually shows.* That interpretive skill is what separates an agent who has data from an agent who understands the market.

The agent with market literacy can look at a rising median sale price trend and explain why a specific seller's home may not have appreciated at the same rate, read inventory and days on market together to distinguish structural buyer demand from seasonal compression, and read a close-to-list-price ratio to tell a buyer how much negotiating room the current market is actually offering rather than what the client assumes. When price reductions are building in a segment, that agent can advise accurate pricing before the seller has spent weeks on the market learning what buyers already knew.

Clients encounter headlines and assume those headlines describe their home, their neighborhood, and their timing. Market literacy gives you a third option between repeating the headline and dismissing it: explain what it actually measures, then connect the conversation back to the decision the client has to make.

What This Book Is and Is Not

This is not a coaching book, an economics textbook, or a market forecast. It does not explain housing market theory or predict where prices will be in six months. It teaches interpretation: what a specific metric measures, where it misleads, how it fits with other indicators, and how to use it in the decision in front of you.

Read it once to build the interpretive framework. Return to specific chapters when a metric comes up in a pricing conversation, a negotiation, or a client question you want to answer with more precision than "the market is up."

What the Book Covers

By the end of this book, you will be able to read a reported price change and identify whether it reflects genuine appreciation, seasonal timing, a composition shift in what sold, or a thin sample. You will look at an inventory reading and tell whether supply is building or compressing, and what that implies for the next 60 days of negotiation. And you will explain to a seller why the metro-area median does not price her home, to a buyer why a quarterly price drop does not automatically create discount room, and to any client why the headline they read this morning may describe a geography or a transaction mix that has nothing to do with their situation.

The book also covers what drives mortgage rate movement, how new construction data signals supply conditions before they appear in resale inventory, and how to read multiple indicators at once rather than one metric in isolation.

Each chapter covers one concept or metric, teaching what it measures, what it doesn't, and how to use it in a real conversation.

What This Book Is For

- For the agent who can pull any market report in 60 seconds and wants to understand what it actually means
- For the professional who wants to price homes from data rather than intuition, and explain that pricing to clients who have done their own research
- For the team leader or brokerage who wants to raise the market literacy of the people around them
- For anyone who has ever cited a market statistic in a client conversation and felt less certain than they sounded

CHAPTER 01

Why Market Literacy Matters

Agents rarely lose credibility because they could not find a number. By the time the conversation matters, the number is usually already on the table, pulled from the MLS, quoted from a market report, or sitting on a client's phone from a headline or portal search. The failure tends to come a step later, when the discussion shifts from whether the statistic exists to whether it actually belongs to the property, the segment, the timing, or the decision the client is trying to make.

You can hear the shift when it happens. The opening claim sounds firm enough because the number itself is real, then the follow-up question arrives, usually one level more specific than the statistic can carry, and the explanation starts getting softer instead of sharper. What looked like evidence a moment earlier starts behaving more like a shield for an underdeveloped recommendation. The problem is not that the data was invented. The problem is that the advice was leaning on a number that hadn't been matched carefully enough to the question in front of it.

That is where the professional risk sits now. Clients arrive with headlines, portal trends, market summaries, and half-assembled conclusions before you ever sit down with them, which means the hard part is no longer getting the report in front of the client. The hard part is deciding which of those numbers belongs in the conversation, which one is only background context, and how to explain the difference without sounding slippery or defensive.

Access Without Understanding

Market reports became easier to produce long before they became easier to interpret. Clients do not experience your work as a test of whether you can pull a number. They experience it as a test of whether you can turn that number into advice they can use.

A seller asks whether the market supports her price. A buyer asks whether a soft monthly headline means there is room to negotiate harder. Another agent asks whether higher inventory means demand is weakening or selection is simply improving. Each question sounds like it should have a data answer, but the first number on the page is rarely the whole answer, and sometimes it is not even the right place to start.

A correct number can still be irrelevant, incomplete, or badly matched to the question. A metro-wide statistic may describe a broad mix of sales while the client needs guidance on one neighborhood and one property type. A month-over-month move can be pure timing noise while the issue at hand is negotiating leverage over the next two weeks. Rising inventory signals opportunity in one segment and pressure in another. If you cannot separate those uses in plain English, the number works against you instead of for you.

That failure compounds. An agent who starts from the wrong market read is likely to price from the wrong anchor, interpret weak activity too late, and arrive at the price reduction after the market has already delivered the feedback more cleanly than the initial analysis did. By then the listing has sat, the seller has watched the traffic slow, and the conversation has shifted from "Why this price?" to "Why did we miss this in the first place?"

I see the same pressure when I talk with journalists about the housing market. The market is usually messier than the story wants it to be, and a fast news cycle tends to reward the cleanest, sharpest framing available. That does not make the headline false, but it does mean consumers often meet the market through language that has been compressed for attention before it has been interpreted for a decision. Part of the value of market literacy is being able to slow that language back down for them.

A seller might see a market update showing that metro-area median prices are up 8 percent year over year and come into the listing conversation expecting that number to attach directly to her house. The statistic is real, so a weak answer starts by agreeing with it: "The market is up, but your home is different." That sounds evasive because it does not explain why. The stronger answer starts by matching the number to the decision. If the median is being pulled up by a heavier mix of higher-priced, renovated closings while the seller's immediate competition is older inventory with longer days on market and recent reductions, the market isn't weak and her statistic isn't wrong. The statistic describes only the broad market; pricing this property requires a narrower look at condition, segment, and current competition.

That is why access without relevance judgment is not neutral. It produces analysis that sounds informed until the client asks the one question that forces the metric to prove it belongs in the room.

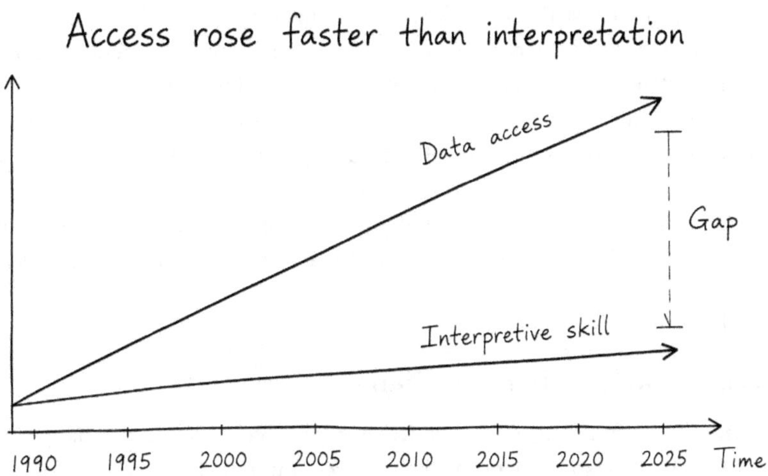

What Market Literacy Looks Like in Practice

A market metric describes something that happened. It does not, by itself, decide what should happen next. Market literacy is the ability to make that second move correctly. You identify what the number actually measures, what question is being asked, and whether the two belong together before you ever try to sound confident about the answer.

That sounds simple until the questions become specific, which is exactly when the skill starts to matter. A rising median may describe the aggregate market accurately while still doing very little to price a particular home. Days on market may describe elapsed time correctly while revealing far less than the showing pattern, price path, and competing inventory do about why the property is sitting. Months' supply may capture market pace at a broad level while still failing to tell a seller whether their segment is tightening or slipping. The agent who reads those distinctions clearly is not showing off technical knowledge. The agent is keeping the analysis attached to the decision.

This is where credibility either strengthens or fails. When you can explain why one number belongs and another does not, the client hears reasoning rather than resistance. When you cannot, the conversation turns into a tug of war between the statistic the client brought in and the recommendation you are trying to defend. One side sounds measurable. The other sounds intuitive. That is not a fair fight.

An agent without market literacy ends up defending the recommendation by feel. "I just think that's what the market will bear." An agent with market literacy can show the work without burying the client in jargon. "That metro-wide number is real, but it is describing a broader mix of sales than the homes you compete with. For your price range, your neighborhood, and the homes buyers will compare against yours this week, *these* are the numbers that actually belong in the pricing decision."

One of those conversations will end in a signed listing. One won't get you a call back, or worse, set you up for failure when the listing hits the market.

What Market Literacy Changes

Market literacy changes the quality of your advice because it changes the quality of your starting point. Pricing recommendations rest on property-level evidence rather than borrowed market shorthand. Timing calls come from indicators that are actually moving in the relevant segment, not from whichever headline happened to circulate that week. And a negotiation position holds up only when the assessment behind it can survive follow-up questions from the other side.

It also changes the sequence of failure inside a transaction. Without relevance judgment, a weak interpretation can sound acceptable at the start because the number itself is real. The problem shows up later. The listing enters too high, showing activity comes in thinner than expected, days on market lengthen, the reduction follows, and the seller starts to wonder whether the market changed or whether the analysis never matched the property in the first place. By the time the price is corrected, the trust problem is larger than the pricing problem.

The benefit works in the other direction too. When you can explain why an average rose because more high-end homes sold, why a monthly dip did not automatically create negotiating room, or why rising inventory did not mean the same thing in every price tier, you are not adding complexity for its own sake. You are removing the wrong conclusion before it becomes strategy. Specificity carries credibility better than confidence alone because specificity shows the client where the reasoning came from.

The effect does not stop at one conversation. A team leader who can distinguish between a useful metric and a distracting one raises the standard of every market discussion around them. A brokerage where agents explain what the numbers mean, rather than repeat them in the order they appear on the report, sounds more serious because the analysis is more serious.

Market Literacy Takeaway

Market literacy is not having more numbers than the next agent. It is knowing which number belongs to the decision in front of you, and being able to explain why.

Use This When

- A client quotes a market headline and applies it directly to their property
- You are pricing a home and the client's price expectation is based on a statistic that may not belong to the property-level decision
- You are writing a market update or positioning a listing and want to sound credible, not just well-researched
- You are negotiating with a buyer or seller who has pulled numbers online and attached the wrong meaning to them
- You need to explain why one correct number is more relevant than another correct number

Be Careful When

- Assuming that data access automatically produces understanding
- Confusing one market statistic with the whole picture
- Applying aggregate metrics to individual properties without first testing whether the statistic belongs to that decision
- Quoting statistics you do not fully understand to justify a position

- Letting a headline statistic drive your pricing or strategy because it sounds objective
- Trying to win an argument with data instead of explaining what the data actually shows

Client Explanation

The numbers you see online may be accurate, but not every accurate number belongs in the decision we are making. A metro-area statistic gives us context, but it does not automatically price your house or tell us how much negotiating room this listing has. For that, I need to look at the segment you actually compete in, the homes buyers will compare against yours, and the market behavior that applies to this decision instead of the market in general.

CHAPTER 02

The Market Is Not One Number

"How's the market?"

In residential real estate, that question gets asked as if it has a single answer and should produce one clean sentence in response. It sounds simple only because the shorthand hides how many different questions are packed inside it. The person asking may be talking about prices, speed, supply, leverage, affordability, timing, or some combination of all of them, while the person answering often reaches for the first statistic that sounds broad enough to cover the ground.

That is usually where the trouble starts. A market question that sounds singular can contain several separate questions, each pointing to a different indicator and sometimes to a different conclusion. Are prices rising? Are homes selling quickly? Is inventory tight? Do buyers have leverage? Do sellers have leverage? Is this a good time to list? Is this a good time to buy? Those are not interchangeable questions, and treating them as if they are is how an agent ends up sounding clear before the analysis has actually become precise.

The problem is not that agents lack market data. It is that "How's the market?" invites a one-number answer to what is, in practice, a multi-part analytical question. By the time you have answered it well, you are no longer answering one question.

Why "How's the Market?" Has No Good Answer

The question "how's the market?" is actually several questions compressed into one:

What are prices doing? How quickly are homes selling? How many homes are competing with mine for the same buyers? What can buyers actually afford right now? Are sellers getting what they ask for?

Each question needs a different kind of evidence, and in any given month that evidence may not point in one clean direction. Prices can still look firm while velocity is slowing. Inventory can rise while desirable options remain limited. Affordability can weaken before closed prices show the strain. That is why a single number cannot carry the whole market conversation.

When a client asks how the market is, they usually mean something more specific. A seller wants to know whether this is a good time to list. A buyer wants to know whether to offer above or below list price. An investor wants to know whether the sales market has moved enough to affect her exit timing. Those are not generic market questions but property-level and decision-level ones, and the answer starts with knowing which indicators are relevant to which decision, in which sub-market.

A single number cannot do that work. Not the median. Not the absorption rate. Not time on market.

The Market Is Many Sub-Markets

The statistic your client found online likely describes a large geography: a metro area, a county, a zip code, an entire state. Markets do not behave uniformly within those different boundaries.

A market can be seller-favored at one price point and buyer-favored at another in the same week, in the same city. The segment priced between $350,000 and $475,000 might carry 8 days on market and close above original list price. The segment above $900,000 might carry 47 days on market and close below original list price. Both exist within "the market." They are not the same market.

Geography does the same thing. Two zip codes two miles apart can show dramatically different inventory levels, velocity, and pricing behavior. School district lines, walkability, proximity to employment, and neighborhood-level desirability create sub-markets within larger ones. A county-level statistic smooths over all of that. What remains is a number that describes every neighborhood a little and no neighborhood accurately.

Property type adds another layer. Condos and single-family homes frequently move at different velocities, respond to interest rate changes differently, and attract different buyer profiles. A market update that combines them into a single figure produces a number that describes neither clearly.

A rigorous market analysis starts by defining the relevant sub-market: the price range, the geography, and the property type that match the listing or the search. Any market summary that skips that step is typically too blunt to be useful.

The Six Market Lenses

The base framework for this book has six market lenses: price, supply, demand, velocity, affordability, and listing performance. No single lens describes the market. Understanding any market requires looking across the lenses together, with each one revealing a different layer.

Price metrics describe where transactions landed. Median price, mean price, price per square foot, and period-over-period price changes tell you where closed sales clustered. They do not explain why. A rising median can reflect genuine appreciation or a shift in the mix of homes that happened to sell. You cannot tell which from the number alone.

Supply metrics describe what is available. Active listings, new listings per month, and total inventory show how many options buyers are evaluating. Low supply tends to favor sellers; rising supply tends to shift leverage toward buyers. Supply metrics are snapshots in time, not trends by themselves.

Demand metrics describe how actively buyers are engaging. Pending sales, showing traffic, and absorption rate reveal whether buyers are moving or waiting. Demand is harder to measure directly than supply because not all buyer activity leaves a data trail. But the delta between active listings and contracts written is one of the clearest demand signals available.

Velocity metrics describe how fast the market is moving. Days on market, days to pending, and close rate show how long it takes a home to move from listed to under contract to closed. Fast velocity and rising prices often appear together. But velocity can slow while prices still show year-over-year gains, which typically means the market is transitioning and recent closed sales have not yet reflected the change on the ground.

Affordability metrics describe what buyers can actually purchase. Mortgage rates, monthly payment calculations, and payment-to-income ratios show the real purchasing constraint. A market can have stable prices and rising supply and still see fewer transactions because buyers who want to own cannot qualify for what is listed. Affordability is frequently the metric agents underweight because it feels macroeconomic and distant from the listing conversation. It is not.

Listing performance metrics describe how individual listings are faring against market expectations. Close-to-original-list-price ratio, price reduction frequency, and reduction magnitude tell you where sellers are meeting the market and where they are not. These are trailing indicators: they describe what closed listings experienced. But they give clear signals about what the current market will absorb.

Later chapters add specialized tools for particular decisions, but these six lenses are the shared vocabulary. They are the default starting point before the analysis becomes more specific.

The Six Market Lenses

Lens	Example Metrics
Price	median, mean, price per square foot, price change
Supply	active inventory, new listings, total inventory
Demand	pending sales, showing traffic, absorption rate
Velocity	days on market, days to pending, close rate
Affordability	rates, monthly payment, buyer capacity
Performance	close-to-list ratio, reductions, reduction size

When Two Metrics Tell Different Stories

Each lens reveals one layer of the market. The harder professional skill is reading what happens when those layers conflict.

Imagine a market where inventory rises from 1.4 months to 2.6 months over a six-month period. More supply is reaching buyers. At the same time, the median price is still reported up 6.4 percent year over year. And days on market has extended from 12 to 26 days.

A seller looking at price reports says: the market is strong. A buyer looking at inventory says: the market is loosening. Both are reading accurate numbers, and neither has the complete picture.

What those three indicators together describe is a market in transition: inventory building, buyers taking longer to decide, but prices not yet adjusted because closed sales are trailing indicators and sellers have not yet recalibrated their expectations. The headline is still showing last quarter's conditions. The underlying market has already moved.

An agent who spots that pattern early can price a listing realistically instead of optimistically, set buyer expectations before the headline catches up, and advise on timing while there is still a meaningful advantage to acting on it.

How to Use the Framework in Practice

The six lenses are tools, not a checklist. The question in front of you determines which ones matter, and starting there produces sharper answers than treating every report as a comprehensive market summary.

If a seller wants to know whether now is the right time to list, the relevant indicators are velocity and supply. How fast are homes moving in her segment? How many listings is she competing against?

If a buyer wants to know whether to offer above or below list price, the relevant indicators are listing performance and demand. What has the market been accepting? Are buyers in this segment competing or waiting?

If a client wants to know whether to expect appreciation over the next year, price metrics alone will not answer the question. Affordability metrics matter too. Prices can rise in an affordability-constrained market, but not indefinitely, and the conditions that end appreciation are visible in the data before they show up in the headlines.

The instinct to answer "how's the market?" with one number is understandable. Clients want a clear answer, not a rigid structure. But a single number only looks like clarity. It is a simplified version of a complicated picture delivered with more confidence than the data supports. The question is not which number to quote. It is which question the client is actually asking and which indicator is built to answer it.

Market Literacy Takeaway

Every market metric answers one question and ignores the rest. Know which question you are actually asking before you pull a number.

Use This When

- A client asks "how's the market?" before a pricing or offer conversation
- You are building a market update and need a framework for which indicators to include
- Two metrics are pointing in different directions and you need to explain why both are accurate
- A client reads a headline statistic that seems to contradict your reading of the conditions on the ground
- You are advising on timing and need to select the right indicators for that specific decision
- The aggregate market number does not match conditions in the specific sub-market you are working in

Be Careful When

- A single statistic is used to justify a pricing recommendation without segment-level analysis
- A market summary covers too broad a geography to be useful for a specific listing
- Different market lenses are pointing in different directions without explanation
- A client applies a metro-level percentage change directly to their own property
- One market lens dominates the analysis because it favors the conclusion someone wants
- The market appears stable in one metric but is shifting in another

Client Explanation

When you ask how the market is, you are really asking several different questions: What are prices doing in your neighborhood? How quickly are homes like yours selling? How many homes are competing for the same buyers? Each question has a separate answer measured by a different set of numbers. I look at all of them before giving you a pricing recommendation or a timing strategy, because the headline number rarely tells the whole story.

CHAPTER 03

Median, Mean, and the Problem of Averages

A seller forwards you a market report. The headline reads, "Median sale price up 7.2 percent year over year." She wants to know why you priced her home at last year's number plus only one or two percent. The math seems obvious to her. The market is up 7 percent, so her house is up 7 percent, and you are leaving money on the table!

You have heard some version of this every quarter of your career. Sometimes it is a buyer running the same logic in reverse. "Average prices fell, so I should offer below comps." Sometimes it is another agent quoting a county figure to justify a list price that has nothing to do with the segment the home is actually in. The mistake underneath all three conversations is the same one. The agent or client is treating a single market average as if it explains the value of a specific home.

It does not. Median and mean both have legitimate uses, and you will use them constantly. But neither one is a verdict on any individual property, and the fastest way to lose credibility with a serious client is to talk as if they are.

What Median and Mean Actually Measure

The **median sale price** is the middle value in a sorted list of closed sales. If you take every home that sold in a market over a defined period, line them up from lowest to highest, and walk to the middle of the line, the price you land on is the median. Half the sales are below it. Half are above it.

The **mean sale price**, also called the **average**, is the sum of all the closed sale prices divided by the number of sales. It is the arithmetic average. If 10 homes sold and you add up their prices and divide by 10, you have the mean.

Both numbers are summaries. Both try to compress an entire market's worth of transactions into a single figure. They do that job differently.

How Each Is Calculated

Median is a position. Mean is a calculation.

Take seven sales in a single month at these prices:
$412,000, $438,500, $455,000, $471,000, $489,750, $512,000, $1,275,000.

To find the median, you sort the list (already done here) and take the middle value. With seven sales, the middle is the fourth one. The median is $471,000.

To find the mean, you add the seven prices and divide by seven.
$412,000 + $438,500 + $455,000 + $471,000 + $489,750 + $512,000 + $1,275,000 = $4,053,250.

Divide by seven and you get a mean of approximately **$579,036**.

The median sits comfortably with the cluster of sales between $412,000 and $512,000. The mean sits more than a hundred thousand dollars above any home in that cluster. Neither calculation is wrong. They are answering different questions.

What Median Tells You

Median tells you where the middle of the market transacted. It is resistant to outliers, which is the technical way of saying that one unusually high or low sale will not move it much. Add a $5 million sale to the dataset above and the median barely moves. Drop the highest sale entirely and the median moves only one position.

That stability is why median is the standard in most market reports. When you read that the metro-area median is $578,000, you are reading where the typical closed sale landed. The metric ignores the outliers by design.

What Mean Tells You

Mean tells you the arithmetic center of all the sales, using every dollar that traded. That is both its strength and its weakness.

Mean is the right number when you actually care about total dollar volume, weighted activity, or how the high end is pulling the rest of the market. If a luxury segment is heating up, the mean will catch it before the median does. If a high-volume builder closes 30 production homes at one price point, the mean will reflect that concentration.

Mean is the wrong number when one or two sales sit far outside the rest of the data. A single $4 million sale in a neighborhood where most homes trade in the high $400s will yank the mean upward by tens or hundreds of thousands of dollars without telling you anything useful about most of the transactions.

How Outliers Distort the Mean

A hypothetical street has ten homes that all sold in the same year.

Home	Sale price
1	$312,000
2	$328,500
3	$341,000
4	$355,750
5	$362,000
6	$378,250
7	$389,000
8	$402,500
9	$418,000
10	$1,675,000

Nine of the ten homes sold in a band between $312,000 and $418,000. The tenth, an unusual property at the end of the street, sold for $1,675,000.

The median sale price is the midpoint between the fifth and sixth homes: $370,125.

The mean sale price is the total ($4,962,000) divided by 10: $496,200.

If you reported the mean as the typical sale price on this street, you would be wrong about nine out of ten transactions. The mean overstates what most homes on the street actually sold for by more than $100,000. The median, by contrast, sits inside the range where the bulk of activity happened.

Now reverse it. Strip the outlier out of the dataset. The mean of the remaining nine sales drops to roughly $365,200, only a few thousand dollars off the median. That is the test. When the mean and the median are close, the data is well-behaved, and either metric is fine. When they diverge, an outlier is doing the work, and you should know why before you quote either number.

In statistics, that divergence is called **skew**. In real estate, skew usually means the sales are not distributed evenly around the middle. A few unusually expensive sales can pull the mean above the median, while a cluster of lower-priced or distressed sales can pull it below. The point is not to turn a

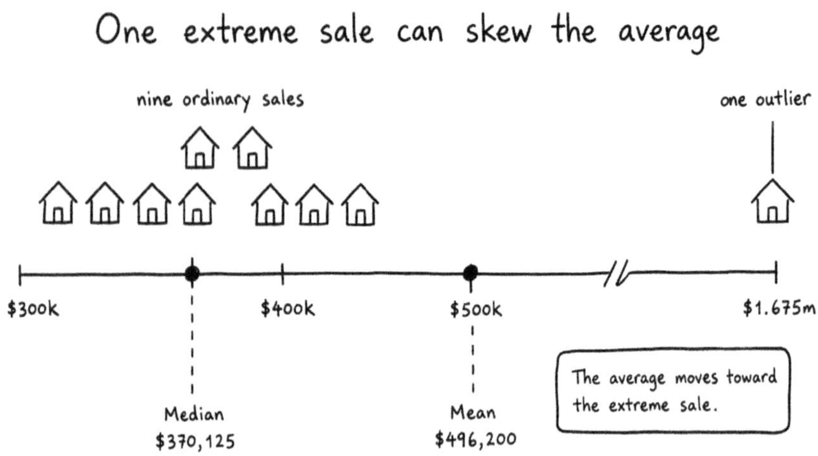

client conversation into a statistics lesson. It is to recognize that a wide gap between median and mean is evidence about the shape of the market, not just a math curiosity.

How a Change in the Mix Can Distort Both

While outliers are an obvious distortion, a harder one to spot is the **composition effect**, sometimes called a **mix shift**. This is when the median or mean moves not because individual homes changed in value, but because the kind of homes that sold changed.

Now consider a second hypothetical: a small market with two segments. In Year One, the market sold the following:

- 40 homes between $300,000 and $400,000
- 10 homes between $700,000 and $900,000

Median sale price for Year One: roughly $365,000.

In Year Two, the same homes are worth the same amounts. Nothing has appreciated. Nothing has depreciated. But the activity mix shifts:

- 25 homes between $300,000 and $400,000
- 25 homes between $700,000 and $900,000

Median sale price for Year Two: roughly $545,000.

The headline number is up nearly 50 percent. The local newspaper writes that prices are surging. A seller in the lower segment reads it and assumes the same increase applies to her home.

She is wrong. Not a single home in the market necessarily appreciated. What happened is that a higher proportion of the sales came from the upper segment, which dragged the median up the price ladder without moving any individual home.

It happens in real markets when a luxury builder finishes a phase of new construction, when interest rate moves push more activity to one tier than another, when a school district draws disproportionate demand for a season, when winter sales skew toward the homes that motivated buyers actually buy. Mix shifts happen silently, and they can move both medians and means.

The number describes only which homes sold.

Why Neither Metric Explains the Value of a Specific Home

Both median and mean summarize a group of sales. The question they answer is: across all the homes that closed in this market during this window, where did prices land? That is not the same question as: what is this house worth?

Pricing a specific home requires property-level analysis: comparable sales of homes like the subject property, in similar condition, in the same location, that closed recently, with adjustments for differences. It requires an understanding of how the market has moved since those comps closed. The market median is context, not a substitute for the analysis.

Most agents know this distinction and skip it anyway, usually when they are tired or rushed. They pull a market trend line, apply it as a percentage to last year's value, and call it pricing. It is not pricing. It is extrapolation from a number that was never designed to answer a property-level question.

How to Use These Metrics in Practice

Use median as your default summary of where most of the market transacted. It is the more honest single number when you have to pick one, especially in segments where a few unusual sales would otherwise pull the average off where the bulk of activity is.

Use mean when total volume or high-end activity is what you actually care about, or when you are pairing the two numbers to show how concentrated the data is. A large gap between mean and median is itself a piece of information. It tells you the data is skewed, usually upward, and that a small number of sales are doing a lot of work.

In pricing conversations, this usually shows up when a seller uses a headline market statistic as a shortcut for the value of her specific home. She sees that median prices are up, or average prices are down, and assumes the figure applies directly to her property. The market statistic describes the sales mix, not the condition, location, features, competition, or buyer response for any individual home.

When you write a market update or build a listing presentation, do three things:

1. Name the geography and the time window. "The Englewood single-family median for the trailing three months is X." A number without a frame is a number without meaning.

2. Quote both median and mean if the gap between them is meaningful, and explain what the gap shows.

3. Separate the market summary from the pricing analysis. The market is the background. The comps are the foreground. Do not let the background do the foreground's work.

When a client cites a market percentage and applies it to their home, do not argue with the percentage. Reframe the question. The market average tells you what the group of sales did, but their home is not the group. Their home is one property, and pricing it correctly requires looking at homes like it, not at an average that includes the entire metro area. That distinction keeps the conversation anchored to evidence instead of letting a broad headline become a pricing model.

Market Literacy Takeaway

Median and mean describe the market. Neither prices the house.

Use This When

- Reading a market report and choosing which summary number to quote
- Translating a county- or city-level statistic for a client who only cares about their neighborhood or segment
- Building a listing presentation that needs to show market context without overstating it
- Writing a market update where median and mean diverge and the gap is itself the story
- Explaining to a client why a percentage change in the market does not apply directly to their home

Be Careful When

- The sample is small enough that a few sales can swing either metric
- One or two unusually high or low sales are present in the data
- The mix of homes that sold has shifted from the prior period by price tier, property type, or geography
- A client tries to apply a market-wide percentage change directly to their own property
- A headline reports a single number with no sample size, time window, or geography attached
- New construction or distressed sales are concentrated in one segment

of the data

Client Explanation

The number in that report is the middle of all the homes that happened to sell last quarter, not a measurement of your home. When the median moves, it can be because individual homes are worth more, or because the kind of homes that sold changed, and you cannot tell the difference from the headline alone. To price your home accurately, we have to look at homes like yours, in your condition, in your location, that sold recently.

CHAPTER 04

The Cyclical Nature of Price

A seller mentions, over the fence, that her neighbor's home listed in August and closed in October at 4.3 percent below original list price, after 38 days on market. She takes this as evidence that the market is slowing. She tells you she is going to wait until spring.

She may be right to wait, but "the market is slowing" is not what the data showed. The data showed a familiar seasonal pattern: homes listed in late summer and closing in fall often sit longer and close below list because the calendar has changed, not necessarily because the underlying market has weakened.

Her neighbor did not sell in a weak market. She sold at the seasonal trough, when buyer activity is lower, competition for attention is higher, and negotiating dynamics shift slightly toward buyers. The seller's waiting strategy may be the right call for other reasons. But her diagnosis is wrong, and if she prices based on that diagnosis, she will either overprice her spring listing or underprice her fall one.

What Price Cycles Are

Residential real estate prices do not move in straight lines. They move through cycles: predictable patterns of activity and price that repeat across seasons with enough regularity to be anticipated.

The most visible of these is the seasonal cycle. In many residential markets, buyer activity follows a reliable annual arc. It builds through late winter and early spring as buyers enter the market after the holidays, peaks in late spring and early summer when weather improves and school-year decisions sharpen, and eases through fall and into winter as buyers defer discretionary moves. New listings often follow a similar pattern: supply concentrates in spring and early summer, thins in fall, and compresses sharply through the holidays.

The interaction of seasonal demand and seasonal supply produces a price pattern most agents recognize intuitively. Prices tend to rise through spring, peak in early summer, ease through fall, and reach a seasonal low in winter before recovering again the following spring. The pattern does not require a weakening market to produce a winter trough, and it does not require an accelerating market to produce a spring peak. The cycle runs on its own logic.

In a stable market with no appreciation and no depreciation, this cycle can still happen. Prices do not sit flat across all 12 months. They move with the calendar.

The Cycle and the Trend

Price data carries two separate movements: the seasonal cycle and the long-term trend.

The seasonal cycle is the annual oscillation. Prices rise in spring, ease in fall, and rise again the following spring. This happens every year in a stable market and continues in a rising or falling one, overlaid on whatever the underlying trajectory is.

The long-term trend is the underlying direction of prices over multiple years. If the market is appreciating, each year's spring peak is modestly higher than the prior year's spring peak, and each year's winter trough sits modestly higher than the prior winter's trough. The trend is visible when you compare the same period across consecutive years and obscured when you compare across seasons.

A market can show prices "falling" from June to November while prices are simultaneously appreciating year over year. Both observations are accurate, but they describe different things. The June-to-November figure captures the seasonal cycle, while the year-over-year figure captures the underlying trend.

The distinction between cycle and trend is clear in the data and harder to explain in a client conversation. A client who sees prices fall from June to November does not know whether to read it as a market shift or a calendar pattern unless someone explains both.

When a Monthly Price Change Misleads

A month-over-month price change does not tell you whether the market is strengthening or weakening. It tells you where in the cycle you are.

Consider a market where median close prices have tracked the following seasonal pattern for four consecutive years:

Period	Approximate median
February	$431,000
May	$469,000
August	$457,000
November	$441,000

From February to May, prices rise 8.8 percent. An agent who quotes that figure in late spring sounds like they are describing an accelerating market. From May to November, prices fall 6 percent. An agent who quotes that figure in late fall sounds like they are describing a correction.

Neither observation is wrong, but both are incomplete. What they describe together is one annual cycle in a market that is not necessarily surging or correcting. The seasonal movement is the recurring structure.

Now run the year-over-year comparison. If the following February's median is $441,000 rather than $431,000, that 2.3 percent gain is real appreciation, stripped of seasonal effect. If it is $421,000, that 2.3 percent decline is real depreciation. The same-period-prior-year comparison is the one that shows market direction. The month-to-month comparison mostly shows the calendar.

Agents, journalists, and commentators who quote month-over-month numbers without naming the seasonal context are not lying, but the result can still mislead. They are presenting one number from a story that requires several to understand. A seller reading "prices fell 6 percent this fall" does not know whether that is alarming or routine unless someone explains the cycle.

What a Real Market Shift Looks Like

The seasonal pattern has a second use: it creates a baseline. When a market deviates meaningfully from its expected seasonal behavior, that deviation is the signal worth reading.

Example: A market has tracked its seasonal cycle reliably for five consecutive years. Prices peak in May and trough in November, within a predictable range. In year six, the spring peak does not materialize. May prices come in significantly below the prior year's May, and buyer activity remains soft through what is normally the strongest selling season. That is not a calendar effect. That is a structural shift, and the seasonal pattern makes it visible precisely because the deviation is clear against the baseline.

The reverse works too. A November trough that lands above the prior year's November, in a market that historically eases in winter, may indicate durable demand that is not following the seasonal pattern. Deviations like that are often the first clue that the market is behaving differently than the calendar alone would predict.

A single month's anomaly might just be noise. A quarter's sustained deviation from the expected pattern is worth tracking. A full cycle of deviation from the historical baseline is evidence of something structural.

This is where agents can do better than the headline. If fall prices are lower than spring prices, the first move is not to call the market weak. It is to ask whether fall usually looks that way. If a spring market fails to produce its usual lift, the first move is not to explain it away as noise. It is to check whether buyer activity, inventory, days on market, and reductions are confirming the break from pattern.

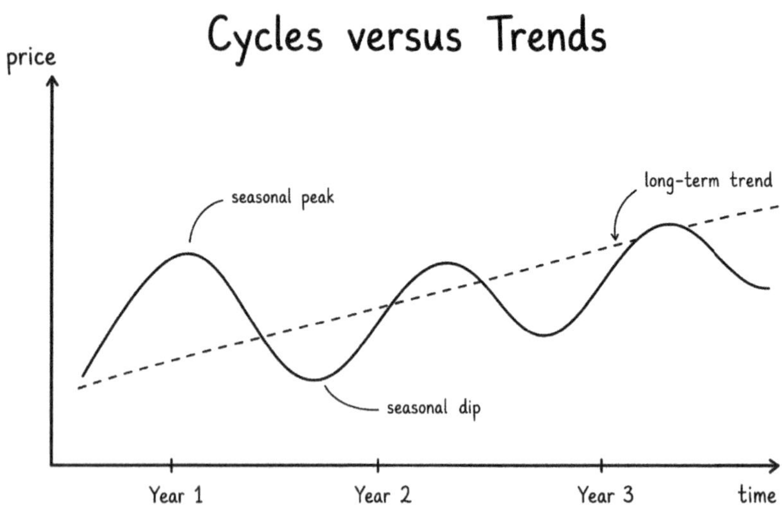

A seasonal dip can exist inside a longer appreciation trend.

How to Use This in Practice

Compare year over year, not month over month. When a client or a report presents a price change, the first question is: which periods are being compared? A May-to-November comparison captures the seasonal cycle. A November-to-November comparison captures the underlying trend. When a client shows you a figure that reads the wrong way, the fastest correction is usually "let's look at the same period last year."

Know your market's pattern. The calendar matters, but local calendars are not identical. School-year timing, weather, tourism, employment cycles, and second-home demand can all change when a market normally peaks or slows. An agent who knows exactly when their local market peaks, when it troughs, and what the typical range looks like is more precise in client conversations than one who applies the generic description.

Use the cycle for pricing strategy. A home listed in November in a market with a pronounced seasonal trough should be priced and positioned differently than the same home listed in April. The November seller is competing for a smaller pool of buyers, likely receiving less traffic, and negotiating against buyers who know the market has cooled. That is not a pricing problem; it is a timing reality. Setting that expectation before the listing goes live is better than explaining it after the first week of low showings.

Set client expectations before they encounter the cycle. When a market enters its seasonal trough, sellers need to understand that slower activity is normal, not alarming. When a market enters its spring surge, buyers need to understand that competition will feel more intense than what they saw in December. Both conversations go better when the agent explains the cycle before the client experiences it.

Market Literacy Takeaway

Price cycles are the calendar. Trendlines are the market. A seasonal dip is not a correction, and a seasonal surge is not a shift.

Use This When

- A client interprets a seasonal price change as evidence of a market trend

- You are pricing a listing in fall or winter and need to explain why recent comparable sales reflect seasonal conditions, not permanent changes in value
- A market report shows month-over-month or quarter-over-quarter price movement and a client wants to know if the market is rising or falling
- You are advising a seller on whether to list now or wait for spring
- A buyer sees a seasonal price trough and asks whether now is the time to negotiate aggressively

Be Careful When

- Comparing prices across different seasons without naming the seasonal effect
- Reading a single month's anomaly as evidence of a structural shift
- Applying the standard seasonal pattern to markets that behave differently (warm-weather markets, resort markets, or markets with local employment cycles that override the typical seasonal shape)
- Assuming that year-over-year gains during a heated demand cycle reflect durable long-term appreciation
- Forgetting that sustained deviation from the seasonal pattern is itself a meaningful signal, not just more noise

Client Explanation

In many residential markets, prices follow a seasonal pattern that repeats every year. They tend to build through spring, peak in early summer, ease through fall, and reach a low in winter before recovering again. A price change that follows that pattern is the calendar, not the market. The comparison that removes the seasonal effect and shows the underlying direction is year over year: how do prices this November compare to last November? That is the figure that tells you whether the market is actually moving, and which way.

CHAPTER 05

Interpreting Price Changes

A reported price change is not an explanation. It is the result of a comparison between two sets of closed sales, and until you know what changed inside those sets, the number tells you less than it appears to.

The arithmetic may be perfectly correct and still be easy to misuse. Most reported price changes compare a summary statistic, usually the median or mean close price, across two periods. That comparison can tell you that the aggregate result moved. It does not automatically tell you that individual homes appreciated, that buyer demand strengthened, or that sellers in a specific segment suddenly gained pricing power.

What produced the movement is the harder question, and it is the one that actually belongs in professional analysis. A reported increase may reflect genuine appreciation, but it may also reflect a seasonal shift in when homes closed, a different mix of price points or property types, a thin sample, a broader geography masking segment divergence, or some combination of those forces at once. The percentage is the visible output. The cause is the part that determines whether the number is useful.

Before you use a price change in a pricing conversation, a market update, a negotiation, or a client explanation, you need to know what produced it. Otherwise a mathematically correct figure starts carrying conclusions it never established, and the analysis moves from measurement into inference without pausing long enough to ask whether the inference is earned.

What a Reported Price Change Actually Measures

A price change report compares a summary statistic (usually the median or mean close price) across two time periods. It describes the aggregate of all closed transactions in both periods. It does not describe what happened to any individual property.

Sale price and **property value** are not the same thing. A market where the median sale price rose 5.9 percent over 12 months has one data point about aggregate transaction activity. It does not tell you that any specific home is worth 5.9 percent more than it was a year ago. It tells you that the collection of homes that sold this year produced a different median than the collection of homes that sold last year, and those collections may not have been comparable in type, condition, location, or price range.

Price is what transacted; value is what a specific property is worth to a buyer in a current market. The two track each other over the long run in healthy markets, but in the short run, the gap between a reported price change and a specific home's actual movement can be substantial.

That distinction matters every time a seller applies a percentage to her estimated value, or a buyer adjusts a negotiating position based on a quarterly figure. The headline is accurate. The inference from headline to specific property is almost never accurate in the exact amount it specifies.

Four Sources of Misleading Price Movement

A reported price change can reflect genuine appreciation or depreciation. It can also reflect any of four other forces, alone or in combination.

Seasonal timing. Most residential markets follow a predictable seasonal price pattern: prices build through spring, peak in early summer, ease through fall, and reach a seasonal low in winter. A comparison that crosses a seasonal inflection point will capture that oscillation as though it were a trend. October-to-November figures will almost always show price easing, regardless of what the underlying market is doing. The fix is to compare the same period in consecutive years (November to November, June to June), which removes the seasonal effect and reveals genuine directional movement.

Composition shift. When the mix of properties selling changes, the aggregate price figure changes even when no individual home changes in value. If luxury sales represent a higher share of transactions this month than last month, the median rises without any real appreciation. If a builder delivers a block of entry-level homes, the median can fall while every property in the market is priced accurately. The same composition effect that distorts median and mean within a single period also operates over time. A price change that reflects what sold, rather than what homes are worth, is a composition artifact, not a market signal.

Sample size. Thin transaction periods produce volatile readings. A market that typically closes 90 homes per month may close 34 in a slow winter month. A single unusually high or low sale in that thin month moves the median more than the same transaction would move it in a busy month. Small geographies face this problem year-round: a zip code or neighborhood with 8 to 12 transactions per month has too small a base for reliable trend data. The number is real. The signal it carries is weak.

Geographic and property type scope. A metro-level price change can conceal dramatically different movement in its sub-markets. A reported metro-area decline may be driven entirely by softening in the luxury segment while entry-level properties are flat or rising. A reported metro-area increase may reflect activity in one growth corridor while other areas are stable. Property type adds the same problem: combining single-family homes and condominiums into a single figure produces a number that accurately describes neither.

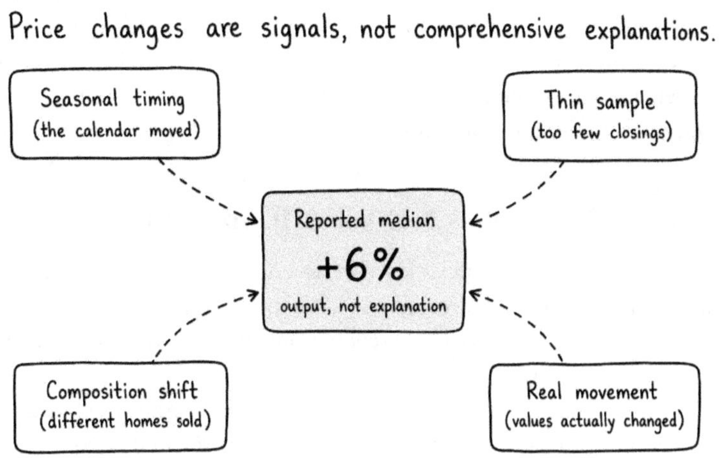

How to Cross-Check a Price Change

A reported price change, by itself, is a single reading from a single instrument. The analysis becomes more reliable when you run it against other indicators.

Inventory tells you whether supply conditions are consistent with the reported price direction. Rising prices alongside rising inventory is less durable than rising prices with contracting inventory. Supply trajectory shapes how long the reported direction is likely to continue.

Days on market often leads price movement. Because close prices are trailing indicators, reflecting deals that went under contract weeks or months earlier, days on market can show you where the market is heading before prices catch up. If days on market is rising while prices are still reported as flat or positive, the price data has not yet reflected conditions on the ground.

Price reductions show seller response to real-time buyer behavior. When the frequency or magnitude of price reductions increases, close prices tend to follow. A market reporting stable or rising median prices alongside a growing share of listings taking reductions is approaching a turning point that the close price data has not yet confirmed.

Together, these three indicators can support or complicate a headline price change. A reported price increase that coincides with falling inventory, stable or improving days on market, and low price reduction frequency is more reliable than a reported increase sitting alongside rising supply, slower velocity, and widening price cuts.

When the Number Is Not What It Appears

Example: A market typically closes between 85 and 95 homes per month with a median close price around $447,000. In March, the reported median jumps to $474,000, a gain of 6.0 percent in one month. The following month it falls back to $451,000.

The 6.0 percent is accurate. The cause: a new condominium building delivered 28 units in March, all priced between $680,000 and $890,000. Those 28 closings, added to the typical 85 to 90 single-family closings, pulled the median up across the combined dataset. The following month, with only a handful of remaining units from that building closing, the median returned near its prior range.

No individual property appreciated 6.0 percent in March. No buyer paid more for a comparable home than she would have in February. What changed was the composition of what closed. The figure was accurate. What it implied was not.

An agent who pulls the transaction detail, identifies the condo delivery, and strips the composition effect from the analysis before advising is doing a different job with the same data.

This is the practical move in a pricing conversation. A seller may bring in a reported metro increase and ask why it does not apply directly to her property. A buyer may bring in a reported decline and treat it as permission to write a weak offer. In both cases, the professional answer starts by separating the reported aggregate from the actual segment, property type, and current competitive set. Do not dismiss the number; keep it in the lane where it belongs.

How to Use Price Changes in Practice

The professional approach to a price change figure is not reflexive skepticism. It is the discipline of asking four questions before presenting or acting on any reported change.

What time period? Month-over-month, quarter-over-quarter, and year-over-year comparisons answer different questions and carry different reliability. Know which comparison you are reading before drawing a conclusion. For trend analysis, year-over-year is the most seasonally stable choice. For tracking a market in rapid transition, shorter periods may add useful context if their limitations are named.

What sample? How many transactions does the comparison rest on? A figure drawn from 14 closings in a slow month in a small sub-market should be described as suggestive, not definitive. If the sample is large and consistent across both periods, the figure carries more weight.

What geography and property type? Is the reported change from the metro area, the county, the zip code, or a specific segment? Are single-family homes and condominiums combined? The closer the geography and property type are to the subject property, the more relevant the figure.

What else is moving? Before presenting a price change, check whether inventory, days on market, and price reduction trends point in the same direction. A price change confirmed by supporting indicators is a stronger finding than one that stands alone.

When explaining price changes to clients, name the denominator explicitly. "Year-over-year median for single-family homes in your zip code" is a specific claim. "Metro-area prices are up" is not. Clients who hear the full description understand why the headline may not apply to their transaction. Clients who hear only the percentage are set up to misapply it.

And when a price change is genuine, year-over-year, supported by consistent indicators, and relevant to the actual sub-market in question, say so directly. The discipline is knowing which numbers hold up and which ones need more scrutiny.

Market Literacy Takeaway

A price change is a signal that requires a source. The source determines the response.

Use This When

- A client reads a price change headline and wants to apply it directly to their listing price, offer, or negotiating position
- You are building a market update and need to present a price figure without overstating certainty
- A reported price change seems inconsistent with what you are observing in active listings and showings
- A buyer uses a reported price decline to justify a below-market offer
- A seller uses a reported price increase to anchor a price above what comparable sales support
- A market report leads with a price change and you need to evaluate whether the figure is reliable before relying on it

Be Careful When

- Reporting month-over-month or quarter-over-quarter changes without naming the seasonal context
- Treating a metro-level price change as applicable to a specific neighborhood, price range, or property type
- Accepting a price figure from a thin transaction month as a reliable trend signal
- Missing a composition shift because you are looking only at the headline number
- Presenting a price change without cross-checking it against inventory, days on market, or price reduction data
- Assuming that multiple consecutive months of movement in the same direction is a durable trend, since seasonal patterns can produce several months of consistent apparent movement in one direction

Client Explanation

That percentage comes from comparing the median price of all the homes that closed this period to all the homes that closed in the comparison period. It doesn't mean your specific home went up or down by that exact amount. Before I give you a price direction to act on, I look at what actually produced the change: whether a different type of home dominated sales this month, whether there were fewer transactions than usual, and whether the same direction holds when you compare the same time of year to last year. If the direction survives those checks, it's something we can act on.

CHAPTER 06

Seasonality, Trendlines, and Headlines

A reader following housing coverage in almost any market cycle will eventually run into headlines that sound something like this:

"Home sales fall from the summer peak."
"Prices remain higher than last year."
"Inventory rises as homes take longer to sell."
"Well-priced listings still attract buyers."

All four can be true in the same market, in the same month, and none of them tells you much by itself until you know the comparison frame underneath it. A month-over-month decline from late summer into fall may be the normal seasonal slowdown. A year-over-year price gain may still be intact at the same time. Inventory can rise because the market is loosening, or because the annual listing cycle has reached its usual autumn shape. A listing can still move quickly inside that slowdown because the segment, price point, and positioning are doing different work than the headline comparison.

That is where the comparison frame starts doing the work. The problem is not that the market information is false. The problem is that headlines, brokerage summaries, and even clean-looking trendlines tend to flatten the comparison period, the seasonal baseline, and the expected annual pattern into one decontextualized number, which makes routine calendar movement read like a market shift and can make a structural market shift look routine if you are measuring against the wrong frame.

The seasonal cycle in price is only the most visible case. Here the question is different. The same calendar logic keeps showing up in inventory, buyer activity, days on market, concessions, and the headlines built from all of them, which means the interpretive problem is no longer simply whether seasonality exists. It is whether the reader knows when a number is describing the calendar, when it is describing the underlying trend, and when it is marking a deviation from the expected pattern.

Seasonality Beyond Price

Price is the most visible market metric, but it is not the only one shaped by the calendar. Once you move beyond price, the risk of misreading the movement often gets worse, because inventory, buyer activity, days on market, reductions, and concessions can all soften together at the same time and create the appearance of a weakening market even when they are mostly following the usual seasonal arc.

Inventory rises and thins seasonally. Buyer activity expands and contracts seasonally. Days on market extends when the buyer pool narrows. Reductions and concessions become more common when sellers keep pricing for the season that just ended. None of that automatically signals deterioration. It may only mean that the market has moved from spring conditions to fall conditions, and the comparison being used has not named the calendar shift underneath the number.

This is where market summaries and headlines start distorting the picture. Measured against the summer peak, the same ordinary fall movements can read like a coordinated breakdown: inventory changing shape, days on market extending, reductions increasing, concessions widening. The numbers are not necessarily wrong. The frame is often too compressed to tell you whether you are looking at normal seasonal movement or a real change in market conditions.

Seasonal Baseline vs. Structural Change

To distinguish a seasonal movement from a structural market shift, you need a baseline: the expected level of a metric for this time of year, drawn from the historical pattern.

A seasonal baseline is not just the average. It is the expected reading for this specific month, in this specific sub-market, given the typical annual arc. November inventory in a market that has averaged 2.1 months of supply every November for the past five years has a baseline of 2.1 months. If this November comes in at 2.0 months, that is noise. If it comes in at 3.4 months, that is worth examining.

The baseline converts a raw number into a deviation. And it is the deviation, not the raw number, that carries the signal.

Example: A market tracks its seasonal cycle consistently across five consecutive years. November closed sales run between 210 and 240 per month every fall. Days on market in November averages 28 days. Active inventory in November averages 1.9 months of supply. Those are the baselines.

In year six, closed sales in November come in at 172. Days on market extends to 44 days. Inventory reaches 3.1 months. Every metric is moving in a direction that looks like a seasonal pattern, but the magnitude is well outside the expected range. The deviation is consistent across inventory, velocity, and price behavior.

That is structural, which the baseline made visible.

A structural change is a sustained departure from the expected seasonal pattern, across multiple metrics, over multiple months. A single month's anomaly might be noise. A full quarter of readings that consistently deviate from the historical baseline, across inventory, velocity, and price behavior, is evidence that the market itself has shifted. The seasonal pattern does not cause confusion. It provides the frame that makes structural shifts readable.

This is also the client-conversation move. When a client says the market changed, you do not have to argue with the feeling. You can place the feeling against the baseline. If the metric is inside its normal seasonal range, the answer is calmer: this is what this month usually does. If the metric is outside the range and other indicators confirm it, the answer becomes more direct: this is not just the calendar anymore.

What Trendlines Reveal

A trendline is a line fitted through multiple data points over an extended period. Its purpose is to surface the underlying direction of a metric, separate from the seasonal oscillation that runs through any annual data.

If you plot monthly closed prices over three or four years and draw a line through the seasonal peaks and another through the seasonal troughs, you can see the underlying appreciation or depreciation rate independently of where you are in the cycle. A market that peaked last May above the prior May, and that troughed last November above the prior November, is appreciating. The trendline makes that visible without requiring you to strip out the seasonal effect manually.

The same logic applies to inventory, days on market, and other metrics. A trendline through five years of November inventory readings tells you whether the seasonal trough is deepening, stabilizing, or rising. That direction is not available from a single reading, and it is not reliably available from year-over-year comparisons that may fall in different phases of a cycle.

A trendline extends backward to explain and forward to project. The projection is where the value shows, and where the risk begins.

Where Trendlines Mislead

A trendline is only as reliable as the data it runs through.

Fit a trendline through data that includes the 2020 and 2021 demand surge and the projection will imply a pace of appreciation the market has already failed to sustain. The base period was anomalous: historically low rates combined with pandemic-era demand concentration in residential real estate produced a price acceleration with no precedent in the preceding decade and no continuation in the years that followed. A line drawn through that period and extended forward is not a projection but a reminder that the base years were exceptional.

Short trendlines carry the same problem. A six-month line in a rising market looks like a permanent trend. A two-year line that begins in a trough and ends at a peak will show a slope the market will not sustain once the cycle turns. The longer the trendline, the more seasonal oscillation it absorbs, and the more reliable the directional signal.

A trendline drawn through an anomalous period overstates direction. A trendline drawn through too short a window may capture a single seasonal cycle rather than an underlying trend. Both produce projections that agents can present as forecasts when they are artifacts of where the endpoints happen to fall.

When presenting a trendline, name the period it covers and whether that period includes any known anomalies. A trendline from 2015 through 2025 is a 10-year market read. A trendline from 2020 through 2022 is a pandemic-era read. Those are different claims about the same market.

Why Headlines Distort

A market headline converts multidimensional, seasonal, context-dependent data into a single statement designed to attract attention.

That compression is not a conspiracy. It is a format constraint. A headline has one slot for a number and one frame. It will choose the number that is largest and the frame that is most newsworthy. "Closed Sales Fall 22 Percent From Summer Peak" is accurate if November closed sales are 22 percent below July. In a market where that July-to-November decline happens every year, it is also routine.

The distortion is not that the number is wrong. It is that the headline strips the comparison baseline before publishing. The reader sees 22 percent without knowing whether 22 percent is alarming or routine. In a market with that historical pattern, it is routine. The reader does not know that.

A headline has to sound clear, timely, and worth clicking before anyone reaches the second paragraph, and the format rewards urgency, contrast, and decisiveness even when the underlying market is not offering a single dramatic conclusion. That does not require bad faith from the writer. It is simply what the format selects for.

Housing markets often resist that kind of clean framing. Inventory can rise while desirable supply remains limited. Prices can still be up year over year while momentum is clearly softening underneath the surface. Buyer demand can be weaker without disappearing. Sellers can have less leverage without buyers taking full control. A seasonal slowdown can be pronounced without marking a structural turn. Several of those conditions can exist at once, which makes them awkward headline material even though they are often the most honest description of the market.

That pressure gets stronger as the news cycle gets faster, and nuance is the first thing squeezed out. A market update that should begin with the comparison frame, the segment, the baseline, and the expected seasonal shape gets compressed into a cleaner statement that sounds more decisive than the data really is. Consumers ultimately bear the cost when that compressed language gets reused as advice.

This is where market-literate agents are useful, not because they are there to argue with the article, but because they can translate it back into the market conditions the headline had to leave out. They can ask which metric moved, compared to what period, in which segment, against what seasonal baseline, and with what actual consequence for the decision in front of the client. The expertise is not in dismissing the story. It is in slowing the interpretation down until the number is attached to the right frame again.

Example: A market closes 310 homes in July. In November, closed sales come in at 242, which is 22 percent below July. A local outlet publishes: "Home Sales Drop Sharply as Housing Market Cools." The story is accurate. What it does not say is that this market has produced a July-to-November decline of between 18 and 24 percent every year for the past six years. It does not say that November-to-November closed sales are actually up 4 percent from last year. It does not say that days on market in November is tracking within two days of the prior November average.

A buyer who reads only the headline has one piece of accurate information and no context for whether it means anything. A buyer who reads it with an agent who knows the seasonal baseline has the same accurate number and a complete interpretation.

The technically accurate headline is not the problem. The missing context is.

How to Read a Headline With a Client

An agent who dismisses a client's headline has closed the conversation the headline opened. Clients who bring in outside information are looking for context, not correction, and that distinction changes how the conversation goes. The approach is not to override what the client read but to supply what the article omitted.

Three questions do that consistently.

What is the comparison? Every market figure compares one period to another. A November figure compared to October shows the seasonal pattern. A November figure compared to the prior November shows underlying trend. Ask which comparison the headline used. If the article does not say, that is itself useful information.

Is this seasonal or structural? Place the reported movement against the historical baseline for that metric at that time of year. A 22 percent July-to-November decline in a market where the average is 21 percent is seasonal. A 22 percent decline where the average is 11 percent warrants examination. The baseline converts a number into a deviation, and the deviation is the signal.

What does it mean for this specific decision? A client who adjusts strategy because sales fell from July to November is treating a seasonal pattern as if it were a market direction signal. The right question is not what changed from summer to fall but whether conditions are improving or deteriorating compared to the same period last year. That year-over-year comparison is what connects a headline to a real decision.

The three-question sequence does not require a proprietary tool or a special report. It requires knowing the seasonal baseline for the key metrics in your market and making it a habit to ask which comparison the headline used before drawing any conclusion from it.

Market Literacy Takeaway

Most short-term market movement is the calendar, not the market. A trendline shows the underlying direction the calendar obscures. Headlines reduce both to a single number without naming which one they are describing.

Use This When

- A client brings in a market headline and wants to change their pricing, timing, or negotiating strategy based on it
- A market report shows a significant change in inventory, days on market, or sales volume and you need to assess whether the movement is seasonal or structural
- You are explaining why buyer activity is lower in fall than in spring without implying the market is weakening
- A seasonal price reduction pattern is making a seller nervous before you have established the baseline
- You are building a market update that uses trailing data likely to be interpreted as worse or better than the underlying trend supports

Be Careful When

- Citing a trendline drawn through an anomalous period as a projection for what the market will do next
- Treating a headline that is technically accurate as a reliable strategy input without supplying the seasonal context it omitted
- Assuming the seasonal pattern you know in one market applies equal-

ly in another

- Presenting a seasonal figure to a client without naming the baseline: the number without the baseline is noise, not context
- Dismissing a client's headline concern without engaging with what it actually shows; clients who feel dismissed become defensive, not open

Client Explanation

What you read is probably accurate as far as it goes. What it usually doesn't tell you is whether that movement is the seasonal pattern, which happens every year and reverses, or a genuine shift in market conditions. Before I advise you to act on a headline, I look at two things: how does this period compare to the same period last year, and is the metric following its normal seasonal shape or deviating from it? Those two checks tell me whether the headline is worth acting on.

CHAPTER 07

The Pricing Path: Original List Price, Current List Price, and Close Price

At her listing appointment, the seller has already found a comp she considers definitive. "That house two blocks over sold for 99 percent of asking," she says. "I want to price mine right there."

You pull the full listing history. The property entered the market at $624,000 in early February. After two weeks with no offers, the price dropped to $599,000. Three weeks passed without a contract. When an offer came in at $587,000, the listing agent adjusted the list price in the MLS to $587,000 before marking the property under contract. It closed at $587,000. Close to final list price: 100 percent. Close to original list price: 94.1 percent. Days on market: 47.

The seller is not wrong to look at comps. She is looking at the number most reporting platforms surface by default: close price relative to the most recent list price. That ratio describes the last day of a 47-day process in which the seller absorbed significant market feedback, gave up $37,000 from the original ask, and watched a listing agent bury the pricing history beneath a reset list price before the transaction closed. To read that sale correctly, you need the full story: where the seller started, how the market responded at each price, and how far the final outcome landed from where the listing began.

The number that tells that story is not the close-to-final-list ratio. It is the close price to original list price ratio, and to understand it you need to understand the four prices that build it.

The Four Numbers

Most closed sales involve four distinct figures, each recording a different moment in the pricing story.

Original list price (OLP) is the price at which the property first appeared on the market. It represents the seller's initial public pricing position: what the seller and their agent believed buyers would accept, or what the seller was willing to test, at the moment the listing went live. It is a hypothesis.

Current/last list price (the final list price once a property has closed) is the most recent asking price before the transaction completed. If no reductions occurred, current list equals OLP. If the listing went through reductions, current list reflects the price the seller reached after the market declined to engage at something higher.

Close price is the price at which the transaction completed. It reflects what one buyer agreed to pay and what one seller agreed to accept at the end of the negotiation.

Close price to original list price ratio (CP/OLP) is close price divided by original list price, expressed as a percentage. It connects the final outcome back to the first public pricing position. A ratio of 100 percent means the property closed at exactly the original ask. A ratio above 100 percent means the market bid the price up. A ratio below 100 percent measures how far the final result landed from where the seller started.

Why Each Number Answers a Different Question

Close price alone tells you where the transaction ended. OLP tells you where it started. Current list price tells you where the seller was positioned when a buyer finally engaged. CP/OLP tells you the total distance between the seller's original expectation and the market's final answer.

These are not interchangeable numbers. A close price of $545,000 describes a fact without context. A close price of $545,000 against an OLP of $600,000 describes a seller who gave up $55,000 from the original ask before finding a buyer. A close price of $545,000 against a current list of $550,000 describes a negotiation that looked clean at the end, while saying nothing about the two reductions that preceded it. All three framings use the same close price. They tell entirely different stories.

How Current List Price Obscures the Pricing Path

Many MLS displays and third-party reporting tools show close-to-list ratio against the current list price at time of contract. That default is not wrong arithmetically, but it omits what happened before the final list price was set. When a property went through one, two, or three reductions before finding a buyer, the final list price reflects where the seller landed after absorbing market feedback, not where they started.

Price shaving makes this problem worse. When a listing agent adjusts the list price in the MLS to the expected close price immediately before going under contract, the published close-to-list ratio becomes 100 percent regardless of how far the property traveled from its original price. The pricing history is not falsified; it remains in the listing detail. But the headline ratio, the one most sellers and agents see in market reports and comp sheets, describes only the last day of a longer story.

When close-to-final-list ratios are calculated across a market with frequent reductions or active price shaving, the aggregate figures can overstate market strength. A segment that consistently shows close-to-list ratios near 99 percent may in fact have sellers who are routinely entering the market above where buyers will engage, reducing twice, and then closing near the reduced final price. The correct denominator for evaluating negotiating dynamics is always OLP, because OLP is the number that has not been shaped by what the market said.

What Price Reductions Signal

A price reduction is market feedback in its most direct form. It tells you that a property was offered at a price, buyers reviewed it, and no one found the combination of features, condition, location, and price compelling enough to make an offer. One reduction after extended market time may reflect an optimistic original price correcting itself. Two reductions over two months is a more sustained signal: buyers repeatedly found the asking price above what they would pay relative to alternatives they had.

Reductions also change the negotiating posture of whatever comes next. A seller who has moved from $600,000 to $550,000 has demonstrated willingness to adjust. A buyer who understands the pricing path enters the negotiation differently than one who sees only the current list price. The pricing path is visible in the listing history, and prepared buyers and their agents look at it.

When reviewing comps for a pricing conversation, the reduction count and reduction pace carry interpretive weight that the close-to-list ratio does not capture. A comp that sold at 98 percent of OLP in 12 days is a different signal than one that sold at 99 percent of a third-round final list after 80 days on market. They may close at similar absolute prices. They describe very different market experiences.

The Calculation

CP/OLP = Close Price / Original List Price

Example: A home enters the market at $600,000. After three weeks with no offer, the seller reduces to $575,000. Two more weeks pass, another reduction: $550,000. An offer comes in at $545,000 five days later. The home closes at $545,000.

Against the current list price of $550,000: $545,000 / $550,000 = 99.1%
Against the original list price of $600,000: $545,000 / $600,000 = 90.8%

Both ratios are accurate. They answer different questions. The 99.1 percent figure describes a negotiation that resolved cleanly against a price the seller had already accepted after two rounds of market feedback. Measuring close price against that number is like grading the test after changing the answer key. The 90.8 percent figure describes the full distance from where the seller started to where the market said the property was worth, across 40 days. That is the figure with interpretive weight.

Now consider two comps in the same neighborhood, both reported as closing near asking price:

Home A: Listed at $512,000. Under contract in nine days. Closed at $498,000. Close-to-OLP: 97.3 percent.

Home B: Listed at $549,000. No offers for four weeks. Reduced to $519,000. No contract for three more weeks. Reduced to $499,000. Under contract in 12 days. Closed at $494,000. Close-to-final-list: 99.0 percent.

The 99 percent on Home B is high precisely because the list price by then reflected everything the seller had already conceded. When calculating CP/OLP across a group of listings, the correct method is to average the individual transaction ratios, not to divide the average close price by the average original list price; the shortcut introduces a small but consistent error that compounds in datasets with wide price dispersion.

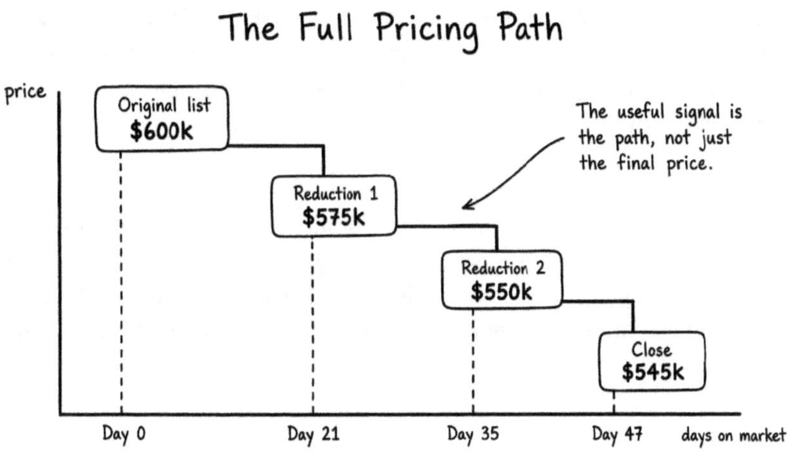

What the Pricing Path Reveals

Taken together, OLP, the reduction history, current list price, close price, and CP/OLP describe four things about any closed transaction.

Pricing accuracy. A listing that moved from OLP to close without reductions and closed near its original ask was priced in the range where buyers were willing to engage. A listing with multiple reductions and a close price materially below OLP entered the market above where buyers would act.

Market feedback. Each price change in the listing history represents a round of market feedback the seller absorbed. The count, magnitude, and pace of reductions show how far the seller's expectations diverged from buyer willingness, and how long it took for the seller to accept the correction.

Buyer leverage. Every reduction already in the record is leverage a prepared buyer can bring to the table. The path is not private: it sits in the listing history and informs every offer from an informed buyer.

Market sentiment. When CP/OLP ratios are tracked across a segment over time, they describe the typical distance between where sellers enter the market and where transactions close. A ratio that sustains above 100 percent signals buyers willing to bid above original asking prices: demand is outrunning supply, or sellers are pricing conservatively relative to what buyers will bear. A ratio that falls materially below the segment's recent norm, across multiple months or a full selling season, signals sellers who are consistently entering above where buyers will engage.

One useful property of CP/OLP is that it is entirely relative. Unlike median close price, which changes as absolute values change, CP/OLP remains interpretable regardless of price level. A 97.4 percent ratio in a market where median prices are $350,000 describes the same negotiating dynamic as a 97.4 percent ratio where median prices are $1,200,000. This means the metric can be compared across time and geography without adjusting for price tier.

What the Pricing Path Does Not Prove

The pricing path is a trailing record. CP/OLP describes transactions that have already closed, not what is happening in current negotiations. Depending on the pace of the market, the ratio may reflect conditions from 30 to 90 days prior. In a market that is shifting, the numbers will lag the present reality.

The path also does not explain cause. A low CP/OLP might mean sellers are overpricing, buyers are constrained by affordability, inventory has increased enough to give buyers alternatives, or broader economic conditions are reducing buyer confidence. Each of those causes produces a similar ratio and requires a different strategic response. CP/OLP signals the pattern. Days on market, inventory levels, and absorption rate explain it.

Small samples distort the ratio in both directions. A segment-level figure built on 11 or 12 transactions can look materially different from the broader market because one or two outlier sales pull the average away from where most transactions settled. Note the sample size before drawing conclusions from any CP/OLP figure.

The practical habit is simple: before you let a comp speak, make it tell the whole pricing story. If a sale looks strong because it closed close to asking, pull the original list price, every reduction, the dates attached to those reductions, and the days on market at each stage. Often the close price is not the surprise. The path to the close is.

How to Use This in Practice

Pull the full listing history on every comp before citing it. Close price and current list price are the first numbers that appear in most MLS displays, but they are not the full story. OLP, intermediate prices, reduction dates, and days at each price stage are all in the listing history. That history is the comp. The close price by itself is one data point.

Use CP/OLP as your primary signal in pricing conversations. A market where most homes close to OLP is a market where well-priced listings find buyers without significant concessions. A market where CP/OLP regularly lands materially below OLP, with frequent reductions, is a market where optimistic pricing has a measurable cost in time and seller concessions. Those are structurally different environments, and close-to-final-list ratios will not distinguish between them.

Show the segment's average CP/OLP to anchor seller expectations. When you show a seller what other sellers in their price tier and property type have actually received relative to where they started, you are quantifying what the market has been accepting. If that average shows a consistent gap between original ask and close price, the practical translation is that the typical seller in this segment has had to absorb that gap before finding a buyer. A seller who prices optimistically should expect to absorb a similar distance, take longer, or reduce before a buyer commits. That framing is more precise than "the market is soft."

Explain the pricing path to buyers before they read the close-to-list ratio. A buyer who sees recent sales at "98 to 100 percent of list" and concludes there is no room to negotiate may be drawing a reasonable inference from incomplete data. If those sales involved multiple reductions before landing at the final list price, the pricing path tells a different story, and the buyer's offer strategy should reflect that.

In market updates, name the denominator. When publishing a close-to-list ratio, specify whether it uses OLP or final list price. The distinction matters more in markets with active reduction cycles, and a market summary that omits it cannot be accurately compared across markets or prior periods.

Track CP/OLP alongside days on market. The two metrics tend to move together: when CP/OLP tightens, DOM usually does too. When they diverge, something worth investigating is happening. CP/OLP falling while DOM holds flat often indicates buyers are negotiating harder even on listings that are not sitting, which can signal affordability pressure the market has not yet priced in to the headline data.

Market Literacy Takeaway

Close price tells you where the market ended. Original list price tells you where the seller started. The distance between them is where the market's judgment lives.

Use This When

- Reviewing comps for a CMA and evaluating whether recent sales reflect clean pricing or extended market exposure with reductions
- A seller anchors pricing expectations to a close-to-list ratio from a market report, another agent's marketing, or a portal search result
- A buyer wants to calibrate an offer and needs to know what the full pricing history of comparable sales shows about seller flexibility
- Writing a market update that tracks negotiating dynamics and you need a metric that stays meaningful across price cycles
- Advising a seller on a price reduction and supporting the case with comp histories that show how reduction timing affected close price
- A market report or comp sheet uses close-to-list figures without naming the denominator

Be Careful When

- The MLS platform or reporting tool does not expose OLP or full pricing history; confirm what data is available before quoting any close-to-list figure
- Price shaving is common in the market; published close-to-list ratios may overstate market strength, and the correction requires pulling OLP directly from the listing detail
- New construction sales are in the dataset; builder pricing mechanics differ from resale and produce CP/OLP figures that are not directly comparable
- A market has experienced rapid appreciation and OLP on comps from six or more months prior may not reflect current pricing dynamics
- The sample is small enough that one or two outlier transactions pull the segment average materially away from where most transactions settled
- Reduction frequency is low but reduction magnitude is large; infrequent steep reductions signal a different dynamic than frequent modest ones

Client Explanation

When you see that a home sold for 99 percent of asking price, the question worth asking is: which asking price? A home that enters the market at $600,000 and closes at $545,000 after two reductions shows 99 percent of its final asking price and 90.8 percent of what the seller originally expected. The number that tells the true story is how far the close price landed from where the seller started, not how close the final list price and the close price were. When the original ask and the close price diverge significantly, the pricing path between them is where the market's judgment about that property lives.

CHAPTER 08

Days on Market and Market Psychology

The listing hit the market with everything in place. Professional photographs, a clean pre-listing inspection, a well-written description, and a yard that showed well in late spring. In the first 10 days, there were 11 showings. Buyers came through. The feedback came back consistently positive on condition and presentation and consistently pointed at one thing: the price.

The seller held. She believed in the home and did not want to signal urgency. Three weeks passed. The 11 showings became 4. Then 2. The feedback from later buyers had a different texture. One buyer's agent asked whether the seller had any flexibility. Another asked how long the home had been on the market, paused, and then asked why it was still available.

The home had not changed. The condition was the same. The photographs were still current. What had changed was the number next to "Days on Market" on every portal and MLS search result, and what that number was communicating to every buyer who clicked through: other people have seen this home, considered it, and decided not to buy it. The listing was still a house. To buyers, it was becoming a question.

What Days on Market Measures

Days on market (DOM) counts the number of calendar days a listing has been actively available for purchase. In most MLS systems, the count begins when a listing is activated and stops when the listing goes under contract. It does not count the days under contract. It does not count days when the listing is withdrawn or expired. It counts the days the property was available and buyers were not buying it.

That definition sounds simple, and in a single transaction it usually is. The complication arises when a listing has been through multiple periods of market exposure.

How It Is Calculated, and Why the Number You See May Not Be the Whole Story

MLS systems handle relisting differently, and the rules govern what the DOM figure on any given listing actually represents.

Active days on market (ADOM) measures DOM within the current listing period only. If a listing expires after 45 days, sits off the market for 30 days, and relists with the same broker, the ADOM counter on the new listing often starts at zero. The prior 45 days disappear from the visible count, even though buyers who searched the area during that period saw the property, formed opinions, and moved on.

Cumulative days on market (CDOM) counts all active market days across listing periods for the same property, regardless of how many times it has been listed, expired, relisted, or changed brokers. This is the figure that reflects total market exposure, and it is the one most useful for understanding what the market has been telling the seller over time.

The difference between the two matters most when a listing has had a troubled history. A property that has spent 90 cumulative days on market across two listing periods but shows a fresh ADOM of 8 looks far newer in a portal search than it really is. Buyers who search the neighborhood and find the property know it is new in the MLS. Buyers who searched the same area two months ago may remember seeing it before.

Back-on-market (BOM) status adds another layer. When a contract falls through and a property returns to active status, some MLS systems restart the ADOM clock. The property has new exposure to buyers who were not in the market during the prior listing period, but it also carries the history of a contract that failed, which buyers and buyer's agents typically notice and ask about.

When you are reading DOM on a comp or an active listing, the first question is which figure you are looking at. If the platform does not show CDOM, pull the full listing history before drawing conclusions.

What Low DOM Can Mean

A listing that goes under contract in the first week or two is often evidence of accurate pricing, strong positioning, adequate preparation, and a market with enough active buyers to meet inventory. In a healthy demand environment with limited supply, well-priced listings tend to find buyers quickly because there are more buyers watching new inventory than there are homes that match what they are looking for.

Low DOM is not, by itself, proof that the seller underpriced. In a competitive market with multiple offers, a home that accepts an offer on day 5 may close at or above original list price. In a slower market, a home that closes in 10 days may simply have been priced at the number where one motivated buyer was willing to act, with no competing interest. The same DOM figure tells different stories in different supply and demand conditions.

What low DOM reliably signals is that the market responded. Someone wanted the property enough to write an offer before significant time passed. Whether that response reflects deep demand, precise pricing, unique features, or favorable timing is a question the other metrics help answer.

What High DOM Can Mean

A listing that has been on the market for 45, 60, or 90 days is telling you something. What it is telling you requires interpretation, not assumption.

The most common cause is overpricing. A seller who enters the market above where comparable closed sales support will find buyer attention without buyer offers. Buyers come through, recognize the price is above what they can justify relative to alternatives, and move on. The listing accumulates days while the price stays put.

Overpricing is common enough that high DOM invites the assumption. But other causes produce the same number. A property with a condition issue that discourages offers at any price above a threshold will sit. A property in a location that limits the buyer pool by geography, commute, school district, or proximity to something undesirable will move more slowly regardless of pricing accuracy. A property type with a naturally smaller buyer pool (a two-bedroom condo in a market dominated by families, or a five-acre parcel in an area where most buyers want turnkey) will take longer to find its buyer than median DOM in that market would suggest.

A market that is softening will also produce higher DOM across the board. If absorption rate is falling and inventory is building, average DOM rises even on accurately priced listings because there are fewer buyers moving relative to the homes available. In that environment, high DOM on a specific listing may reflect market conditions rather than anything the seller or agent did wrong.

Reading high DOM correctly means asking: is this property sitting because of its price, its condition, its location, or the market it is in? The DOM number alone does not tell you which. Showing data, buyer feedback, and the absorption rate in the relevant segment do.

Why DOM Is a Psychology Metric, Not Just a Market Metric

Sellers experience market time emotionally. Each week that passes without a contract is a week of uncertainty, of carrying costs, of holding their own life in suspension. The home they are trying to sell is still the home they know, and the number on the screen does not change what they believe about it.

Buyers experience market time as information. A listing that has been on the market for 35 days has been seen by other buyers who did not buy it. Those buyers may have had good reasons that had nothing to do with the property's value. Or they may have found the price too high, the condition too uncertain, or a competing option more appealing. The buyer looking at the listing on day 35 does not know which of those explanations is correct. What the buyer does know is that the property has had market exposure and has not been absorbed. That is a fact, and it affects how the buyer approaches the decision.

The question buyers ask in the first days a listing is available is: is this home right for me? The question buyers ask about a listing that has accumulated significant time is: what is wrong with it, and how much leverage do I have? While the property has not changed, the question has.

The First Market Window

When a listing activates, it appears as new in every portal search result, every saved search notification, and every active buyer's feed. Buyers who have been searching a specific area, price range, and property type for weeks or months get an alert. Their agents see the new listing come through on the morning report. The listing receives a burst of concentrated, voluntary attention from the buyers most likely to be ready to act.

This first market window is the period of maximum buyer attention, and it is not replaceable. It does not recur. A price reduction three weeks into a listing brings some renewed attention, but it is not the same attention: the buyers who have already seen the listing and moved on will not return with the same energy they brought to a new listing. Some will return. Many will not. The new attention the reduction attracts is from buyers who were not yet looking, which is a smaller and often less motivated pool than the buyers who were already active.

A seller who prices too high entering the market and hopes to reduce later is making a specific trade: they are exchanging the peak buyer attention they would have had at an accurate launch price for a second-chance window that arrives with fewer buyers, more accumulated skepticism, and a listing that carries visible history.

The cost of overpricing is not simply extra time on market. It is the loss of the buyers most likely to pay the most, because those buyers were in the market at the moment the listing was overpriced and have already made their decision.

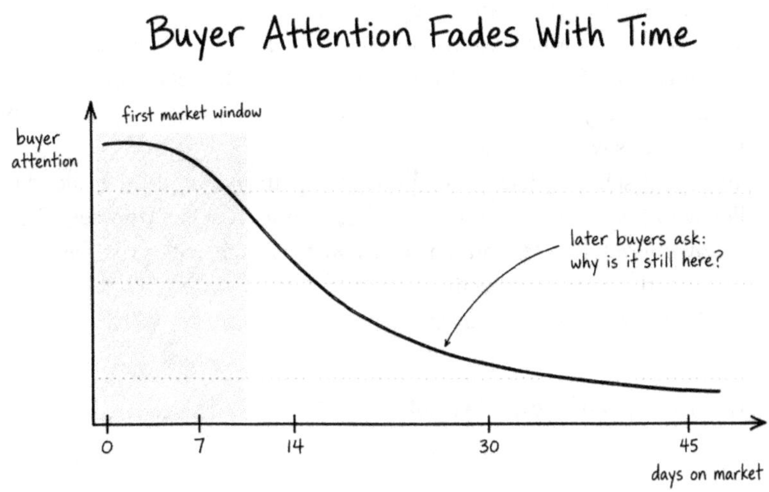

Two Listings, One Neighborhood

Example: Two similar homes in the same neighborhood list within a week of each other.

Home A lists at $487,000, a price consistent with recent comparable sales. In the first six days, the listing receives nine showings and two offers. The seller accepts the stronger offer. Home A goes under contract at $492,000 on day 6.

Home B lists at $519,000 in the same week. The sellers believe their home is worth more than recent comps suggest, and their agent agrees to test the price. The first week brings eight showings. No offers. The feedback is consistent: buyers like the home but cannot justify the price relative to what has recently closed. The sellers hold. Week three brings three showings. Week four brings two. On day 28, the price drops to $489,000.

Four days after the reduction, a serious buyer tours Home B for the first time. Their first question to their agent: why did it reduce and how long has it been on the market? The agent explains that it was overpriced and the seller has come down. The buyer makes an offer at $478,000, citing the extended market time as part of their rationale. The sellers counter. After negotiation, Home B closes at $483,000 on day 45.

Home B took 45 days: two weeks of strong activity that produced no contract, a price reduction, and a negotiation the buyer opened by pointing to the DOM. Home A needed just six days. The $9,000 difference between the two outcomes does not capture the full cost to the sellers of Home B: additional mortgage payments, carrying costs, and weeks of uncertainty while their plans were on hold.

This is why seller updates should show the pattern, not just the calendar. A seller who hears "we are at day 28" hears time. A seller who sees first-week showings fall into second- and third-week silence, with price feedback repeating underneath the decline, sees market response. DOM becomes useful when it is attached to buyer behavior.

How to Cross-Check DOM

DOM does not diagnose itself. When a listing is accumulating days without a contract, the question is why, and DOM alone cannot answer it. The cross-check requires looking at several other indicators together.

Showing activity by week is the most direct companion to DOM. A listing with ten showings in week one and zero in week four is telling a different story than a listing with two showings per week across four weeks. Declining showing traffic suggests buyers have seen the listing and decided against it, which points to price or condition. Consistent low traffic from the start may indicate a positioning or presentation problem, or a limited buyer pool for the property type.

Price reduction history shows when and how often the seller has already responded to market feedback. A listing with two reductions and high DOM has been progressively meeting the market. A listing with no reductions and high DOM has not yet absorbed what the market is communicating.

Absorption rate in the segment establishes the baseline. If the segment is absorbing 35 percent of available inventory per month and a listing has been on for 60 days without a contract, the listing is underperforming the market. If absorption is 8 percent and 60 days is close to the average, the listing is performing normally within a slow market. DOM is only meaningful relative to what the market is doing around it.

Concession requests and feedback from showings can confirm what DOM is suggesting. If multiple buyers have toured and left feedback about price, that is a market verdict. If buyers are citing condition, the issue is different and a price reduction alone may not resolve it.

How to Use DOM in Practice

Before a listing goes live, explain the first market window. A seller who understands that the first two weeks carry disproportionate buyer attention will approach the launch price differently than one who assumes pricing can always be corrected later. The framing is not that overpricing is always a disaster, but that the buyers most likely to be competitive are the ones who see the listing when it is new. Setting that expectation before launch gives the seller a framework for understanding why the launch price matters more than the eventual list price.

During seller updates, use showing traffic to interpret DOM. Week-over-week showing counts tell the seller whether the market is responding to the price as set. A decline in showings after the first week or two is normal. A sharp drop early, or showing traffic that never materialized at all, is a signal worth addressing proactively rather than waiting for the seller to ask.

When recommending a price reduction, connect the reduction to DOM, not just time. "You've been on the market 30 days, let's reduce" tells the seller about time. "You've had 14 showings with consistent price feedback, and the buyers most motivated to act in this neighborhood have already been through and moved on; the next wave is going to start from a lower reference point" tells the seller about leverage. The second conversation gives the seller a reason to act before the accumulating DOM costs them more than the reduction would have.

For buyers evaluating a listing with high DOM, use it as context, not as a lever. An offer that opens with "we are offering less because you've been on the market 45 days" is likely to alienate a seller who has not yet accepted that the time on market reflects a pricing problem. An offer structured at a price the market supports, supported by comparable sales analysis that shows what properties like this one have actually closed for, is more likely to result in a negotiation than one that leads with the DOM as a negotiating point.

In market reports, track average DOM by segment as a directional indicator. Average DOM rising in a specific price tier, while inventory is building and absorption is slowing, is an early signal that the supply-demand balance is shifting before sale price data reflects it. The agent who notices DOM trending up six weeks before a meaningful price adjustment in the segment can advise clients on timing and positioning before the headline data arrives.

Market Literacy Takeaway

Days on market measures how long a listing has been available. What accumulates alongside that count is buyer perception: the question shifts from whether the home is right for them to why it has not sold yet.

Use This When

- Pricing a listing and explaining to the seller why the launch price determines which buyers you reach at peak attention
- A seller wants to test the market at a price above comps before reducing
- Reviewing comps for a CMA and evaluating whether similar homes sold quickly or required extended exposure before finding a buyer
- A buyer is considering an offer on a listing that has been on the market for an extended period and wants to understand what the seller's position likely is
- Writing a market update where average DOM is shifting in a specific segment and you need to explain what that shift means

Be Careful When

- Comparing DOM figures across MLS platforms without confirming whether each reports ADOM or CDOM; the same property's history can look very different depending on which figure is shown
- A property type naturally takes longer to sell due to a smaller buyer pool (luxury, unusual configuration, agricultural, large acreage) and extended DOM is normal for the category
- A listing has returned to active status after a contract fell through; the visible ADOM may have reset while the CDOM and the property's full market history have not
- Using DOM as the sole explanation for a listing's situation without cross-referencing showing data, feedback, condition, absorption rate, and comparable sales in the segment

Client Explanation

The first days your home is on the market are when it gets the most attention from active buyers. They have saved searches. Their agents are watching new inventory. That attention is concentrated, and it fades as the days add up. Buyers who have already seen your home and passed on it will not come back with the same motivation they had when it was new. The buyers who come through at 45 days have a different question than the buyers who came through at day 5: they want to know why no one else has bought it yet, and they will factor that into what they offer. Pricing accurately at launch is about reaching those peak-attention buyers when they are most likely to compete.

CHAPTER 09

Price Reductions and Market Feedback

The sellers did what you recommended. Three weeks ago they reduced the price, and since then the listing has done nothing: no new showings worth mentioning, no offers, the same quiet as before. Now they have their conclusion ready. "We already came down, and it didn't change anything. It's not the price."

They are half right. The reduction did not change anything. What they misunderstand is why. A cut from $588,000 to $579,000 looked like a meaningful move to them and vanished into the noise on the buyer's side. The buyers who saw the home at $588,000 and passed did not come back for $579,000, and no new group of buyers entered a search they were not already running. The reduction was too small to function as a test of anything.

A price reduction is not a single binary event that either works or doesn't. It is a message aimed at a specific set of buyers, and whether it reaches them depends on how far it moves and when. It can be too small to change anyone's math, too late to reach the buyers who were watching, or exactly enough to bring the home back into the conversation. The sellers feel every dollar they give up, while the buyers they are trying to reach may not feel any of it.

What a Price Reduction Is

A **price reduction** is a formal revision to the asking price of an active listing. The change is recorded in the MLS and reflected on every portal carrying the listing within hours. Every buyer who has saved the search or set up an alert gets notified. Every active buyer's agent who has been watching new inventory in that area and price range sees the change flagged.

The mechanics are simple, but the strategic meaning may not be.

Why Price Reductions Are Market Feedback

Most sellers experience a price reduction as a concession: they are giving something up, and the decision often carries the emotional weight of admitting that the original price was wrong. That framing is understandable, but it reverses the actual sequence.

The reduction does not create the feedback. It responds to it. The buyers who toured and did not offer, the consistent comments pointing at the same number, the showing traffic that peaked in the first week and then thinned: that is the feedback. The market communicated, through the behavior of buyers comparing this property to everything else they could buy at the current price, that the asking price was not where it needed to be. A price reduction is what happens when the seller decides to answer.

Reading a reduction as market feedback means asking what the market said before the reduction happened, not just noting that the reduction occurred. A seller who reduces after four days and two showings because she is anxious about carrying costs is in a different situation than a seller who reduces after two weeks, nine showings, and consistent feedback pointing at the same price concern. The reduction looks the same in the listing history. The market verdict behind it is entirely different.

What a Reduction Can Reveal

A price reduction can reflect several different conditions, and distinguishing between them is part of reading a listing accurately, whether it is your active listing, a comp in a pricing conversation, or an active competing property your buyer is considering.

The most common cause is a launch price set above where buyers in the current market would engage for this property, given its condition, location, and competing alternatives. This does not require dramatic overpricing. A seller who enters the market 5 to 8 percent above what recent comparable sales justify will find buyer attention without buyer offers: buyers come through, recognize that the combination of features, condition, and location does not justify a price premium over what has recently closed nearby, and move on without writing.

A reduction can also reflect softening demand at the segment level. A property that would have attracted competitive offers at its current price six months ago may sit today not because the price is wrong relative to historical comps but because the pool of buyers willing to compete at that price tier has contracted since those comps closed. The reduction is responding to where demand is now, not where it was when the comparable sales were made.

Condition or presentation problems produce a similar pattern. When deferred maintenance, inspection concerns, or a layout issue limits the buyer pool at any price above a certain threshold, buyers tend to describe the problem as price because price is the one variable the seller controls. The reduction addresses the symptom; the underlying cause may require a different kind of response.

A change in the competitive set can also prompt a reduction. New inventory listing at a comparable price, a neighboring home that recently sold below this one and is now anchoring buyer expectations lower, or a competing listing that just reduced: any of these can shift the reference point buyers use to evaluate the subject property without the property itself changing at all.

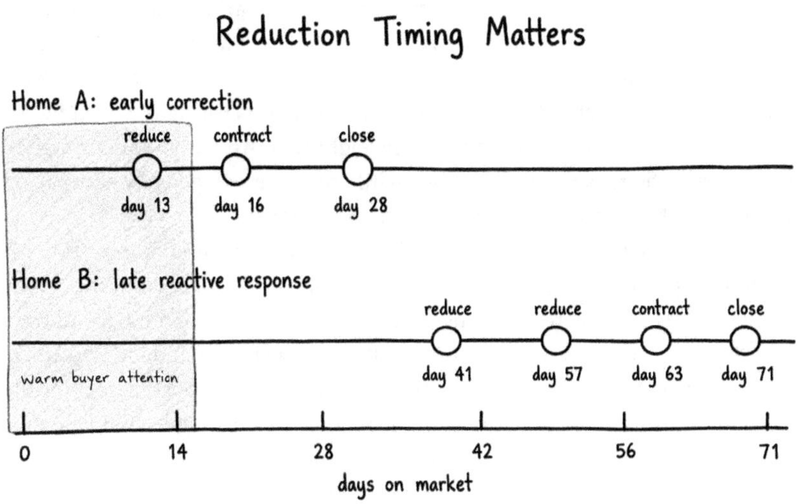

What a Reduction Does Not Prove

A price reduction does not prove the property has a hidden defect. Buyers who toured and did not offer were making a comparative judgment across the available inventory, and their decision not to write says as much about the alternatives as about the property itself.

A reduction does not signal seller desperation in most cases. One reduction from a well-considered launch price, arriving after a coherent cycle of market exposure, is not the same signal as three reductions across 90 days of accumulating market time. Treating all reductions as equivalent misreads the context that makes the difference interpretable.

And a reduction does not guarantee that the new price will work. The revision corrects the listing's position relative to what buyers have been saying, but whether it corrects it by enough, whether the new number lands in a range where buyers in the current market will write offers, is something only the next round of exposure can answer. A reduction sets a new test. It does not pass it.

Timing: Early Strategic Correction Versus Late Reactive Response

The timing of a price reduction often matters more than its size in determining what the reduction can accomplish.

An early reduction, arriving within the first two to three weeks while the listing still carries fresh buyer attention, meets the market in a different state than one arriving after extended accumulation. The buyers who received an alert when the listing went live, who saved it and toured it in the first week, have not yet fully settled into the conclusion that this listing is priced incorrectly for the long term. Some are still weighing it. An early reduction gives them a specific reason to reconsider while they are still actively comparing rather than having already committed to a direction.

A late reduction, arriving after 45 or 60 days of visible market time, is working against the narrative the listing has already built around itself. The active buyers who were watching when the listing launched have had time to compare, decide, and move to alternatives or wait. The reduction attracts new attention from buyers who were not yet looking, a pool that is typically smaller and often less motivated than the buyers who were already active. It also arrives carrying the accumulated weight of DOM, which shifts the question buyers ask about the property, as discussed in Chapter 08.

The practical implication is that there is a measurable cost to waiting.

A seller who holds at the original price for four weeks, hoping for an offer while showings thin, and then reduces because traffic has dried up has exchanged the most valuable buyer attention she had for a second-chance window that arrives with less leverage, more accumulated skepticism, and a listing that has already told a story.

Size: Token, Threshold-Crossing, and Meaningful Repositioning

Three categories of reduction behave differently in the market, and the distinction matters when advising a seller on how much to move.

A **token reduction** is small enough that it does not change buyer math or cross any search filter boundary. Reducing a $598,000 listing to $593,000 produces a change in the MLS activity feed and may trigger an alert for buyers who saved the listing, but the buyers who evaluated the property at $598,000 and did not offer are unlikely to return for $593,000. A token reduction signals that the seller is aware the price needs to move without demonstrating that it has moved to where buyers are actually waiting. The most common outcome is continued market time with a slightly lower number attached.

A **threshold-crossing reduction** is designed to appear in a different set of buyer searches. Many buyers set search filters at round numbers: $500,000, $450,000, $400,000. A reduction from $512,000 to $499,000 moves the listing from searches capped at $500,000 into searches including up to $500,000, exposing it to a pool of buyers who may never have seen it at the higher price. Whether those buyers are the right match for the specific property is a separate question, but the reach effect can be strategically meaningful in a segment where buyer volume is concentrated just below a threshold.

A **repositioning reduction** is large enough to change the listing's competitive set materially. Moving from $519,000 to $487,000 in a market where the $490,000 to $510,000 range has sparse recent activity but the $475,000 to $490,000 range has several recent closings and active competing listings is a different kind of decision than moving from $519,000 to $509,000.

The property is no longer competing against the same alternatives it was at launch. The reduction is not just a new number. It is a new competitive position, and the strategy behind it should reflect where the buyer activity actually is, not where it was hoped to be.

How Reductions Interact with Showings, DOM, and Negotiation Leverage

Price reductions and accumulated market time move together, and buyers read the combination as a single data point about the listing's history and the seller's current situation.

A reduction that arrives on day 14, before the listing has built a visible trail of market exposure, gives buyers a different starting frame than one arriving on day 58. The listing that reduced at two weeks is recent, active, and responding to early feedback. The listing with reductions at day 31 and day 58 has a documented pattern of asking for prices the market declined, and buyers factor that pattern into how they position their offers and what they believe the seller will accept.

Showing activity is the companion metric for reading whether a reduction is addressing the right problem. A listing that received substantial showing traffic in the first week with consistent price feedback has a clear signal: buyers engaged with the property and told you what was stopping them. A price reduction that responds to that feedback directly has a specific audience to reach. A listing that never attracted meaningful showing traffic despite strong preparation may have a positioning or presentation problem that a price reduction alone will not solve, and a reduction made in that environment may simply produce a lower price without a materially better result.

Negotiation leverage shifts with reduction history. A buyer who makes an offer on a listing that has reduced once after an active first two weeks is in a different position than one making an offer on a listing that has reduced three times across 70 days of accumulating market time. The latter buyer often opens with a lower anchor and expects more flexibility, not because the property is worth less in any fundamental sense but because the listing's history signals that the seller has learned, in a public and documented way, that the market is not where the seller originally believed.

Two Listings, One Week, Different Decisions

Example: Two similar three-bedroom homes in the same subdivision list within the same week.

Home A launches at $473,000. In the first 11 days, the listing receives nine showings. The feedback arrives consistently: buyers like the home, and most note that comparable recent sales in the neighborhood support a price closer to $455,000. On day 13, with two of the showing agents having indicated that their clients could revisit at a lower price, the sellers reduce to $458,000. Three days later, they receive an offer. Home A closes at $451,000 on day 28.

Home B launches at $499,000 in the same week. The sellers believe the home's updated kitchen and larger lot justify a price above what has recently closed nearby. The first week brings seven showings. No offers. The sellers hold. Week three brings two showings. Week five brings one. On day 41, the price drops to $479,000. Showing traffic does not return to the prior level. On day 57, the price drops again to $459,000. A buyer who was not yet active in the market when the listing first appeared sees the newly reduced listing, notes the prior price changes in the listing history, and makes an offer at $438,000, citing the extended market time as part of the rationale for opening below the recent reduction. After negotiation, Home B closes at $445,000 on day 71.

Home A closed for $451,000 in 28 days after one early reduction that arrived while buyer attention was still warm. Home B closed for $445,000 in 71 days after two reductions, a first market window that passed without a contract, and a negotiation in which the buyer's opening position was shaped in part by the listing's documented history. The $6,000 difference in close prices does not capture the six additional weeks of carrying costs, nor does it capture the full leverage transfer that accumulated market time produced before the final offer was made.

This is the distinction to make in the seller update. The recommendation is not "reduce because time passed." It is "reduce because the buyers most likely to act have already compared the home to the market, and their behavior is consistent."

How to Use This in Practice

In seller updates, present the market evidence before the recommendation. A reduction recommendation delivered without the supporting data reads as pressure. The same recommendation delivered after walking the seller through the showing count, the feedback pattern, and the trajectory of traffic week over week reads as a response to evidence. Sellers who see the pattern before they hear the recommendation are in a different frame for accepting it, and more likely to accept the size that the feedback actually calls for rather than negotiating toward a token adjustment that does not move the listing where buyers are.

When sizing a reduction, work from the competitive set rather than from what feels like a significant move. The question is where the property needs to be priced for buyers who are currently active and buying comparable homes in this segment. That answer comes from recent closed sales, current competing inventory, and any threshold effect that would meaningfully expand the buyer pool at the new price. A reduction that lands the listing at $497,000 in a market where comparable sales cluster between $490,000 and $505,000 reflects a more careful read than one that produces $494,000 because it felt like a substantial cut.

Frame the reduction to the seller as a response to buyer behavior, not as a concession. The seller who understands that six buyers looked at her home, compared it to every available alternative, and consistently said the price was above where they would act is absorbing market information. The seller who hears only that she is taking less money is absorbing a loss. Those two framings of the same decision produce different outcomes in the room: one leads to accepting the reduction the market is asking for; the other tends to lead to negotiating the reduction down to a number that still does not solve the positioning problem.

When advising buyers on a listing with a reduction history, let the comps carry the argument. A buyer who opens a negotiation by citing "two price reductions" as the explicit justification for a low offer is likely to offend a seller who believes, at the current price, that the property is now fairly positioned. A buyer who structures an offer at what comparable sales support, citing those comps directly, is using market data as the argument rather than the listing's history. The reduction history is relevant context for the buyer's internal read of the situation. It is rarely the right script for the opening of a negotiation.

Before citing a close price from a comp with a reduction history, read the full pricing path. A comparable sale that closed at $527,000 after two reductions from an original list of $579,000 describes a very different seller experience than one that closed at $527,000 from an original list of $534,000. Both are accurate close prices. They describe different interactions between seller expectations and market response, and they carry different weight in a pricing conversation. The close price on its own, without the path that produced it, understates what the data actually shows.

Market Literacy Takeaway

The market delivers its verdict through showing traffic, buyer feedback, and days without a contract. A price reduction is the seller's public acknowledgment of that verdict. Timing determines the result: whether buyer attention is still present to receive the correction, or whether the listing has already absorbed the cost of being wrong first.

Use This When

- A seller is holding at an original list price despite consistent feedback pointing at price, and the case for a reduction needs to be built from market evidence rather than agent pressure
- Reviewing comps for a CMA and evaluating whether a close price reflects clean pricing or extended exposure with reductions before the final contract
- A buyer is considering an offer on a listing with a reduction history and wants to understand what that history signals about the seller's current position and negotiating flexibility
- Advising a seller on how large a reduction to make and when to make it, relative to the listing's DOM trajectory and remaining buyer attention
- A market update includes price reduction frequency as a directional indicator, and you need to explain what an increase in that figure signals about supply-demand balance
- A listing has been on the market with no reductions and no offers, and you need to open the conversation about what the market has been saying and has not yet been answered

Be Careful When

- A listing never attracted meaningful showing traffic despite solid preparation; in that case the problem may be positioning, presentation, or a naturally limited buyer pool rather than price alone, and a reduction may not change the outcome materially
- The reduction is token-sized and does not change the competitive set or cross a meaningful search filter boundary; a small cut that does not reposition the listing relative to buyer alternatives rarely changes buyer behavior
- Multiple reductions have already occurred and significant DOM has accumulated; at that point the negotiation leverage has often shifted substantially to buyers, and the dynamics of the conversation are different from a first-reduction decision
- New inventory has entered the segment at a lower price point since the original launch; a reduction sized to respond to the original feedback may need to be larger to account for how the competitive set has changed
- The buyer pool for the property type or configuration is naturally small, and slower market time may be a function of limited demand rather than overpricing

Client Explanation

When buyers tour your home and leave consistent feedback about price, that feedback is the market's real-time response to your current position. It is not a criticism of the house. It is buyers comparing your home to every other option they can buy at your price, and telling you that the combination of features, condition, and location does not quite clear the bar at the current number. A price reduction is not giving something away. It is acknowledging what those buyers already communicated and repositioning the listing so that buyers can engage while their attention is still on your home. The difference between reducing early, while the buyers who saw the listing at launch are still considering it, and reducing late, after weeks of visible market time have accumulated, is the difference between meeting the market when it is still paying attention and chasing it after it has moved on.

CHAPTER 10

Price Per Square Foot and Its Problems

Price per square foot looks objective because the arithmetic is clean. Take one sale price, divide it by one square-footage figure, and the market appears to tell you exactly what each foot of a home is worth. The ratio can be carried out to two or three decimal places, and that kind of precision can make the result feel scientific, as if the calculation has revealed a clean statistical truth. But more precise arithmetic does not necessarily create a more precise conclusion.

The trouble starts in the denominator. Square footage is not a neutral block of interchangeable space, and the number attached to it is often carrying far more weight than the ratio admits. A square foot above grade does not compete in the same way as a square foot of finished basement. A square foot in an efficient layout does not deliver the same utility as a square foot trapped in awkward circulation space. A square foot in a renovated home on a stronger lot is not doing the same pricing work as a square foot in a dated home whose condition and setting ask the buyer to discount the whole property before the calculation even begins.

That is why price per square foot can be useful as a comparison tool and still fail as a valuation method. The ratio works best when the homes being compared are genuinely similar and the denominator is measuring substantially the same kind of space in both properties. The moment the comparison asks that denominator to absorb different space types, different utility, different condition, or different land value, the apparent precision remains while the analytical value starts to break down.

What Price Per Square Foot Measures

Price per square foot ($/SF) is a ratio: the close price of a home divided by its gross living area (GLA).

$/SF = Close Price / Gross Living Area

The result tells you what a buyer paid for each square foot of measured living space in a completed transaction. As a sorting tool for orientation, it is useful. As a valuation method for individual properties, it is incomplete, and the source of some of the most persistent pricing errors in residential transactions.

The metric is intuitive, which is part of its appeal and part of its problem. It feels mathematical and objective: two homes, two numbers, and the lower number wins. That logic holds when everything except size is identical. In practice, almost nothing except size is ever identical.

How It Is Calculated

The formula is simple. A home closes at $540,000. The MLS shows 1,800 square feet of gross living area. Price per square foot: $300.

The complication begins with the denominator. Gross living area is not a universal figure. Different MLS systems, appraisers, and markets handle it differently. In many markets, finished below-grade space is excluded from GLA and measured separately. In others, it may be included. A home with 1,400 square feet above grade and 600 square feet of finished basement may be listed at 2,000 square feet in one market and 1,400 square feet in another, depending on local convention and how the listing agent entered the data.

When the denominator changes, the ratio changes, and a comparison between two homes using $/SF assumes both denominators are measuring the same thing. They frequently are not.

What It Means

In its best use, $/SF provides a quick orientation to a market or a segment. A buyer new to an area can look at the $/SF range for recently sold homes in a target neighborhood and understand roughly what the market has been paying for size. An agent tracking $/SF over time in a specific product type and geography can observe whether the market is paying more or less per foot than it was six or twelve months ago.

At the segment level, $/SF trends can reveal useful information. If the ratio in a specific price tier has compressed from $310 to $285 over a 12-month period while median prices have held steady, the market may be paying for more size without increasing absolute prices. That is a useful observation about what buyers are getting and what sellers have been delivering.

Where $/SF loses precision is in the comparison of individual properties, because the metric treats every square foot as equal, and no two square feet are ever equal.

What It Does Not Mean

The square footage of a home is a count of measured space. What that space is worth depends on what it is, where it is, how it is organized, and what condition it is in. None of those factors appear in the $/SF ratio.

Location within a geography. Two homes in the same zip code with identical GLA may sell at meaningfully different prices because one backs to a greenbelt and one backs to a commercial property. Both will show a $/SF figure. Neither figure explains the difference. Using $/SF to compare them implies the locations are equivalent when they are not.

Lot size. A 1,600 SF home on a 0.4-acre lot and a 1,600 SF home on a 6,000 SF lot share a GLA figure. They do not share a value. Lot size does not appear in the $/SF calculation. In markets where land matters to buyers (rural properties, homes with view premiums, lots with development potential), using $/SF as the primary comparison metric systematically ignores the component of value that may be doing most of the work in the price.

Layout and utility. A 2,000 SF home with an open floor plan, four bedrooms, and a functional flow has more buyer utility than a 2,000 SF home with chopped-up rooms, a bedroom without a closet, and an addition that added square footage without adding livability. The $/SF figure is the same. The product is not. Buyers choose homes based on how they can use the space, not on how many square feet appear on the certificate of occupancy.

Condition and finish. A home at $300/SF with a fully renovated kitchen, replaced mechanicals, and no deferred maintenance is a different product than one at $300/SF with original 1990s systems, surface cosmetics, and a roof at the end of its useful life. The ratio describes what closed. It does not describe what the buyer will spend after closing.

The above-grade discount. Above-grade square footage often commands a premium over finished below-grade space because buyers value natural light, ceiling height, and grade-level living space differently. A $/SF comparison between a home whose GLA includes finished basement and one whose GLA is entirely above grade is comparing two different types of square footage as if they are equivalent. The buyer who runs that comparison and concludes the basement-heavy home is the better deal may be making the right choice for other reasons, but $/SF did not prove it.

The size-tier problem. Smaller homes often show a higher $/SF than larger ones. A 1,000 SF condo at $400,000 is $400/SF. A 2,500 SF single-family home at $700,000 is $280/SF. A buyer who concludes the condo is overpriced relative to the house has misread the comparison. $/SF is only a stable comparison tool within a narrow size range, in a defined product type, in a consistent geography. The moment a comparison crosses size tiers, property types, or geographies, the ratio is no longer measuring the same thing in both homes.

A Comparison That Does Not Hold

Example: A buyer is evaluating two homes in the same subdivision listed within the same week.

Home A is listed at $549,000 with 1,750 square feet above grade. The home has been updated: new kitchen, new flooring, replaced roof and HVAC. Price per square foot using the MLS figure: $314.

Home B is listed at $529,000 with a total MLS square footage of 2,100 square feet. Pulling the listing detail: 550 of those square feet are finished walkout basement space. Above-grade living area: 1,550 square feet. The basement is finished but below grade, with lower ceiling height and window wells rather than full windows. The mechanical systems are original. Price per square foot using the MLS figure: $252.

By the MLS number, Home B is the better deal by $62 per square foot. By any other measure, the comparison is more complicated. Home A has 200 more square feet of above-grade living space, updated systems, and no deferred maintenance. Home B costs less and offers more square footage on paper, but 550 of those feet are below grade, space an appraiser will value at a discount and a future buyer's agent will need to explain at resale.

The buyer who leads with $/SF will anchor on $252 and $314 and conclude the choice is obvious. The conversation he actually needs is about what the two homes deliver relative to what he is paying, not what each home charged per counted square foot.

The practical fix is to stop the ratio before it becomes the anchor. Pull the listing detail, separate above-grade from below-grade space where the distinction matters, check whether lot, condition, and layout are doing work the ratio cannot see, and then decide whether the $/SF comparison still holds. When it fails, it is rarely because the math is wrong. It fails because the homes were never comparable in the first place.

How to Use Price Per Square Foot in Practice

Use $/SF for orientation and trend-tracking, not for individual property valuation. The metric earns its place in a market update that tracks how the price-per-foot relationship has shifted over time in a specific segment. A 12-month chart of $/SF in a narrow geography and product type is a useful directional indicator. A single $/SF figure used to justify a pricing recommendation is one data point, not an analysis.

When presenting comps, specify what is included in GLA. If one comp has 1,800 square feet all above grade and another has 2,200 square feet including 400 square feet of finished basement, note the distinction before calculating $/SF. A comp sheet that mixes GLA definitions produces ratios that appear comparable and are not. The adjustment does not need to be precise to be useful: even noting "below-grade space not included in GLA" flags the distinction for the client and prevents the comparison from anchoring incorrectly.

Name the variables $/SF cannot carry. Lot size, location within a subdivision, condition, and layout do not appear in the ratio. In any pricing conversation where one of these factors is material, say so before presenting the $/SF figure. A seller with a larger-than-typical lot may be inclined to price at a $/SF premium over comps with smaller lots and conclude the math supports it. It does not, and explaining why requires going outside the ratio.

Correct the size-tier comparison before it anchors the client. A buyer comparing a 1,100 SF condo to a 2,600 SF single-family home using $/SF will almost always conclude the single-family home is the better deal by the ratio. That conclusion is not wrong about the ratio; it is wrong to use the ratio for that comparison. Before a client runs those numbers, frame what $/SF can and cannot do across product types.

In seller conversations, present $/SF alongside the comp's full context. A close-at-$320/SF comp from nine months ago in different condition may or may not support a current pricing position. The ratio does not carry the condition, the timing, or the market trajectory. Present it as one input among several rather than as the answer to a pricing question.

Market Literacy Takeaway

Price per square foot is arithmetic. Valuation is judgment. The ratio tells you what one buyer paid per measured foot; it cannot tell you whether the two homes were ever comparable.

Use This When

- A buyer is ranking homes by $/SF across different sizes, product types, or GLA compositions
- A seller is pricing a listing by applying a $/SF figure from comps without accounting for lot size, condition, or above-grade vs. below-grade square footage
- A comp analysis includes properties with different GLA definitions that affect the ratio materially
- A market update tracks $/SF trends over time in a narrow, consistent segment as a directional indicator
- A buyer or seller is treating $/SF as a valuation method rather than one of several inputs

Be Careful When

- GLA definitions differ across comps in the analysis; mixing above-grade-only and total-including-basement figures produces ratios that cannot be directly compared
- The comparison crosses product types (condo vs. single-family, townhome vs. detached); $/SF is not stable across property types
- Lot size is a material value driver for the properties being compared and does not appear in the ratio
- The size range of the comps spans more than a few hundred square feet; smaller homes generally sell at higher $/SF than larger ones, and the spread can produce a misleading comparison
- A $/SF figure comes from a comp several months old in a market that has moved meaningfully since that transaction closed
- The buyer or seller has already anchored to a $/SF figure as the conclusion of a comparison rather than as a starting point for one

Client Explanation

Price per square foot tells you what buyers have paid for each measured square foot in recent sales. It is useful for understanding roughly where the market is and for spotting outliers. What it does not tell you is whether the square footage in one home is equivalent to the square footage in another, whether lot size or condition or location affected the price, or whether the comparison holds across different sizes or property types. Before using a price-per-foot figure to justify a pricing or offer decision, we check what it includes, what it excludes, and whether the comparison actually holds.

CHAPTER 11

Inventory and Market Velocity

At the Monday team meeting, the market report is on the screen. Active listings in the metro area are up 31 percent from the same week last year. An agent near the back asks whether she should advise all her sellers to price conservatively going in. An agent two seats down says his last three listings went under contract in 11 days. A third says hers has been sitting for sic weeks. They are all looking at the same report.

The headline figure describes the total supply available to buyers at a point in time. What it does not describe is whether different segments of that supply are moving at different speeds, whether the inventory is building because new listings are entering faster than buyers are absorbing them or because existing listings are stalling, or whether the increase will persist or reverse when the season shifts. A rising active count can signal a loosening market, a healthy surge of spring supply, a specific segment that has outrun its buyer pool, or a correction in seller expectations that needed to happen months ago.

Inventory is the count. What matters analytically is what that count is doing, and how fast.

What Inventory Measures

Active inventory is the number of residential listings available for buyers to purchase at a given point in time. It is pulled at a specific moment, usually the last day of the month, and represents the supply side of the current market snapshot. When an agent or a market report says "inventory is at 1,400 listings," that is the number of homes actively available for purchase on that date, not under contract, not closed, not expired.

Inventory is a clear window into near-term market direction when it is read correctly. The challenge is that the count alone does not tell you whether inventory is stable, building, or clearing, and the difference between those three conditions changes everything about how to advise a client.

A Single Inventory Number Is Just a Snapshot

A market with 400 active listings in March and 400 active listings in September may look identical in a report that only shows the active count. If the March market entered the month with 320 listings, added 200 new ones, and generated 120 contracts, it closed the month with roughly 400 listings and absorbed a substantial share of available supply while doing so. If the September market entered with 370 listings, added 80 new ones, and generated 50 contracts, the ending count is similar but the dynamics are entirely different: fewer listings entering, fewer buyers choosing, and accumulation beginning to build underneath a number that still reads as stable.

While the snapshot contains useful information, the motion behind it is the analysis.

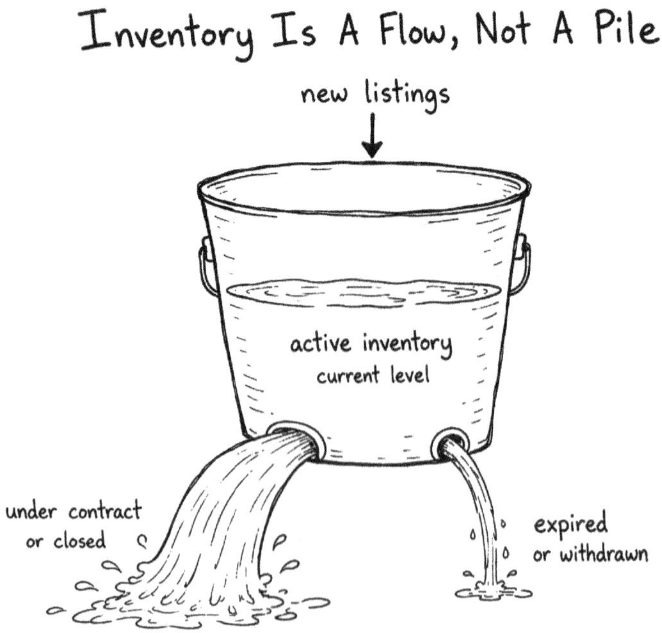

The Flow Underneath

Inventory is the level in the tank, and several distinct flows determine whether that level is rising or falling.

New listings are the input: homes entering the market each period. New listing volume shows whether supply is growing, stable, or shrinking. In spring, new listing volume typically surges as more sellers enter the market, which is why inventory often builds even in strong demand environments. In fall, fewer sellers list, and the input side of inventory naturally compresses regardless of what buyers are doing.

Active listings are the current count: everything on the market that has not yet gone under contract. This is the inventory figure most reports lead with, and it is the level in the tank, not the flow.

Pending sales are the most direct real-time signal of buyer demand. When a listing goes under contract, it moves from active to pending. The count of pending sales in a market, compared to active inventory, shows what share of available supply buyers are actively choosing. A market where pending sales represent 40 percent of active inventory is absorbing supply aggressively. A market where pending sales represent 8 percent of active inventory has buyers looking but not committing in volume, and the relationship between those two numbers tells a cleaner story than either one alone.

Closed sales confirm what pending activity predicted. A closing is the completion of a transaction and the final exit of a property from the inventory system. Closed sale volume, tracked month over month and year over year, shows whether absorption is accelerating, holding, or declining across a longer window than pending activity alone can show.

Expired and withdrawn listings are the exits that do not result in a sale. A listing that expires reached the end of its listing agreement without a buyer. A listing that is withdrawn was pulled by the seller before expiration. Both forms of departure reduce the active count without representing market absorption, and in a market where expired and withdrawn rates are rising alongside a rising active count, the interpretation is fundamentally different from one where listings are exiting primarily into contracts.

What Market Velocity Measures

Market velocity is the pace at which listings move through the market. It is not one number but a reading that comes from the relationship between several:

- How quickly are new listings going under contract relative to how quickly new listings are entering?
- What is the days-on-market distribution for listings that sold versus listings that are sitting?
- What share of active inventory is under contract at any given moment?
- Is the pending-to-active ratio rising, stable, or falling compared to the prior month and the prior year?

A market with high velocity absorbs listings quickly. New supply enters and meets buyer demand before accumulating into a growing backlog. A market with low velocity allows listings to stack: new supply enters but buyers are not keeping pace, and the active count grows even as individual transactions still occur.

Velocity is most useful as a directional signal. The question is not what the velocity is today but whether the market is absorbing supply faster or slower than it was three months ago, and whether that direction is a seasonal pattern or something structural.

How a Market Can Have More Inventory and Still Move Quickly

A rising active count is frequently interpreted as weakening demand. This reading is sometimes correct. It is also sometimes exactly backward.

In a healthy spring market, new listing volume surges as sellers enter ahead of peak buyer season. If buyer demand is rising at the same time, both sides of the inventory equation are active: more listings coming in and more contracts being written. The active count may rise for several weeks because the input is temporarily higher than the output, but the market is not weakening. It is moving. The headline figure, "inventory up 18 percent from last month," describes the input, not the absorption.

The diagnostic question is whether pending activity is keeping pace with new supply. If new listings are up 18 percent and pending sales are also up in roughly the same range, the absorption rate is largely holding and the inventory growth reflects a busier market, not a softer one. If new listings are up 18 percent and pending sales are flat or declining, that gap is the supply-demand signal worth tracking.

How a Market Can Have Low Inventory and Still Feel Weak

Low active inventory is typically associated with seller-favorable conditions. When fewer homes are available, buyers have fewer alternatives, and competition tends to push prices and reduce concessions. This relationship holds when buyers are willing and able to compete.

When buyers have pulled back, whether because affordability is constrained, because mortgage rates have risen enough to narrow the buyer pool meaningfully, or because economic uncertainty has made buyers reluctant to commit, even a low-inventory market can produce slow absorption. Listings sit not because there are too many of them but because the buyers who would normally compete for them are waiting.

In that environment, inventory may be low by historical standards while velocity is also low. The count tells you there is not much available. The velocity tells you that what is available is not moving quickly. Those two signals together describe a market in which supply and demand have both contracted, not one in which sellers hold an advantage. A seller who prices optimistically in a low-inventory market with slow velocity has read the count without reading the motion.

How Seasonality Affects Inventory

Seasonal compression in inventory is one of the most consistently misread market signals. In many residential markets, active inventory declines through fall and into winter not because homes are selling faster but because fewer sellers are listing. The input side of the inventory equation contracts: fewer new listings enter, fewer pending sales are generated, and the count falls without buyer demand having done the work.

A low November inventory figure in a market that routinely shows low November inventory describes the calendar, not the market. A market that shows low November inventory and also shows pending activity consistent with or above prior Novembers may genuinely be absorbing supply well. A market that shows low November inventory and below-normal pending activity has fewer homes available and buyers who are not choosing many of them, which is a thinner market with slow velocity, not a tight one.

When interpreting any inventory reading, the seasonal baseline matters. What is normal for this market at this time of year? The deviation from that baseline, not the raw number, carries the signal.

Two Neighborhoods, One Count

Example: Two neighborhoods in the same metro area each show 50 active listings at the end of the month.

Neighborhood A: During the month, 40 new listings entered the market. Of those and the prior active listings, 38 went under contract within the month. Average days on market for homes that sold: 11 days. The net result: 50 active listings, high throughput.

Neighborhood B: During the same month, 12 new listings entered the market, of which 6 went under contract. Of the existing active listings, 9 expired without a sale. Average days on market for homes that sold: 34 days. The net result: also 50 active listings, low throughput.

Both neighborhoods show 50 active listings. A market summary that stops at the active count finds no difference between them. Neighborhood A is absorbing supply as fast as it enters. Neighborhood B has listings available that the market is not choosing, and the 9 expirations are an additional signal that the gap between seller expectations and buyer willingness has not closed.

This is the point to make before inventory becomes a slogan. If the count is rising, ask whether new supply is entering and clearing, or whether listings are accumulating because buyers are not absorbing them. If the count is low, ask whether buyers are competing for what exists, or whether supply and demand have both gone quiet. The active count starts the conversation. Velocity decides what the count means.

How to Use Inventory and Velocity in Practice

In pricing conversations, use pending-to-active ratio as the lead indicator alongside the active count. The number of active listings tells you how much a seller is competing against. The share of those listings that are currently under contract tells you whether those competing listings are being absorbed. A segment where 35 percent of active listings are under contract presents a different competitive environment than one where 8 percent are, and the difference matters more for pricing strategy than the count itself.

In seller updates, show the week-over-week velocity of the relevant segment, not just the headline inventory number. A seller who understands that 14 homes entered her price range this month and 13 went under contract has a different frame for the market than one who hears only that metro-area inventory is up. The absorption evidence makes the pricing conversation specific rather than general.

In buyer strategy, distinguish between a tight market and a fast market. A tight market has few options available. A fast market absorbs those options quickly. When both conditions are true simultaneously, buyers need to evaluate new listings promptly and structure offers to reflect the competition. When a market has low inventory but slow velocity, the buyer has more time to evaluate and often more room to negotiate. Conflating the two conditions produces the wrong offer strategy in both directions.

When building a market update or presentation, lead with the relationship between new supply and absorption. A headline that says "inventory is up 23 percent from last year" without noting whether pending activity is up or down, whether the increase reflects more listings entering or listings sitting longer, or whether the absorption rate has held, provides one variable from a multi-variable system. Reading it completely requires knowing whether the market is generating more supply that buyers are absorbing or generating the same supply that buyers are passing on.

When comparing inventory across time periods, check whether the change is a flow change or a level change. A market where inventory rose because new listings surged is different from a market where inventory rose because pending activity collapsed. Both produce the same active count. Only one signals that buyer demand has weakened, and they call for different strategic responses.

Market Literacy Takeaway

Inventory tells you what is available. Velocity tells you whether the market is building supply or clearing it. The count alone is a photograph; the motion is what gives it meaning.

Use This When

- A market report shows inventory rising and a seller asks whether she should price conservatively before even listing, without knowing whether the relevant segment is absorbing supply at a normal rate
- A market shows low inventory and a buyer assumes competitive conditions, but the velocity data suggests buyers are hesitant and absorption is slower than the count implies
- Building a market update and need to explain whether an inventory change reflects demand conditions or supply conditions
- Advising a seller on timing and need to show not just how many listings are competing but how quickly comparable listings have been going under contract
- A specific price range or neighborhood is moving at a different velocity than the metro-area headline suggests, and the distinction affects the listing or offer strategy

Be Careful When

- Reporting inventory numbers without specifying the segment; metro-level inventory may be rising while a specific price tier is clearing supply quickly, and the two stories require different advice
- Interpreting seasonal inventory compression as a demand signal; in most markets, November and December inventory declines are a calendar condition, not evidence that buyers are active
- Using the active count without the pending-to-active ratio; the count describes what is available, not whether buyers are choosing it
- Comparing velocity across different seasons without adjusting for the seasonal baseline; a February with the same absorption rate as the prior February may be strong while a February that is above its own prior-year level may be exceptional
- Treating expired and withdrawn listings as equivalent to pending sales in the absorption calculation; they represent failed demand, not successful absorption, and a rising expiration rate is a distinct and more concerning signal

Client Explanation

How many homes are for sale right now gives you one number. What I also look at is how quickly homes in your price range are going under contract, how many new listings are entering the market each month, and what share of the available supply buyers are actually choosing. A market with a lot of homes for sale can still be moving quickly if buyers are keeping pace with that supply. A market with few homes for sale can still move slowly if buyers are hesitant. Before I advise you on pricing or timing, I need both numbers, not just one.

CHAPTER 12

Supply, Demand, and Housing Market Mechanics

Inventory is rising. There is still a housing shortage.

Both statements can be true at the same time, and the apparent contradiction usually comes from one word doing too much work. In housing commentary, supply may mean the homes currently listed for sale, the narrower set of listings that actually compete for the buyers in front of you, or the much larger stock of homes that exists in the market whether those owners have any intention of selling or not. Once those meanings are collapsed into one interchangeable term, the market starts sounding inconsistent when it is really being described at different levels and on different timelines.

For-sale inventory is the count of homes available to buy right now. Available supply is narrower still: the portion of that inventory that is realistically positioned for current buyers at current prices, rates, and property preferences. Housing stock is the full number of homes that exist in the market, most of which are not for sale this week and may not be for sale this year. Structural shortage belongs to that longer horizon. It describes a housing system that has not produced enough homes, over time, to meet the households that need them, even when the listings currently on the market are sitting longer than expected.

A market can have more listings than it had last year and still remain structurally undersupplied. It can also have a structural shortage and still produce stale listings, price reductions, and hesitant buyers if the homes that are available do not match what the current buyer pool can afford or is willing to choose at current prices and rates. Supply and demand are useful only after you define which supply and which demand you are talking about, because in residential real estate, that definition is not a technicality. It's where the analysis starts.

What Supply Means in a Residential Market

To read a market usefully, supply has to mean something more specific than "homes exist." **Available supply** is the number of homes actively listed for purchase and realistically competing for buyers at a given time.

That definition excludes most of the housing stock. Most homes that exist are not for sale in any given month. They are occupied by owners who are not selling, occupied by renters in long-term leases, vacant but not offered to the market, or held by owners under circumstances that prevent an active listing. Total housing stock is a background condition. Active listings are the market.

Available supply is shaped by:

- **Seller willingness**: whether current homeowners are motivated to list, which depends on their financial position, their next housing move, their price expectations, and the opportunity cost of leaving their current home
- **The lock-in effect**: owners holding mortgages at rates substantially below current market levels face a meaningful financial cost to selling; their monthly payment on a replacement home would rise even if they bought at the same price, which reduces the incentive to list
- **Price expectations**: sellers who believe the market will improve in their favor may wait; sellers facing life events act regardless of conditions
- **New construction**: newly built homes that enter the market or compete as alternatives to resale
- **Life events**: relocation, death of a spouse, divorce, retirement, household formation, and similar circumstances that override financial disincentives

When supply is low, the reason matters as much as the fact. A market with low active listings because few sellers are willing to list at current conditions is different from one with low inventory because there are genuinely few properties. Both show the same count. They respond to different forces and require different interpretations.

What Demand Means in a Residential Market

Demand needs the same discipline. In residential real estate, **able demand** is the number of buyers who are both willing and financially capable of completing a purchase at current prices, rates, and conditions.

Wanting to own a home and being able to buy one at current prices are not the same thing, and the distance between those two conditions is where demand analysis earns its practical value.

Able demand depends on:

- **Income and employment**: buyers need qualifying income and stable employment to secure financing
- **Mortgage rates**: rates determine the monthly payment at any given purchase price and set the upper limit of what a buyer with a given income can borrow
- **Down payment capacity**: the cash a buyer can bring to closing determines which price ranges are accessible
- **Price levels**: in markets where prices have risen faster than incomes, the pool of buyers who can afford median-priced homes contracts even if the desire to own has not changed
- **Household formation**: new household formation creates structural demand independent of sentiment
- **Confidence and timing**: buyers who are uncertain about employment, relationships, or plans may wait even when they are financially capable of acting

When demand is described as strong, the relevant question is whether the buyers who want to purchase are actually able to complete transactions at current prices and rates. A market can have large numbers of people who want to own homes and a comparatively small pool of buyers who can act today.

Willing Versus Able: Why the Distinction Matters

A common misreading of demand treats desire as demand. Plenty of people intend to own eventually, but that intent is not active demand, which requires the financial capacity to close a transaction at current prices and rates.

When mortgage rates rise significantly over a short period, the pool of able buyers contracts without any change in the desire to own. The same income and down payment now qualify for a smaller loan, which places fewer available homes within reach. If prices do not fall in proportion to the rate increase, the gap between wanting to buy and being able to buy widens, and transaction volume falls even as the desire to own remains unchanged.

This mechanism explains why a market can simultaneously have low inventory, sellers who want to transact, and buyers who want to own, while still producing fewer transactions at slower velocity. The count of homes for sale and the expressed interest in buying both exist. The able demand that can actually close deals has contracted.

Inventory Is Not the Same Thing as Housing Stock

The opening distinction matters in practice because housing commentary routinely compresses short-term inventory movement and long-term housing scarcity into the same conversation, then leaves the reader to sort out whether those claims belong to the same timeline. They usually do not.

For-sale inventory can change week to week as new listings enter, homes go under contract, and sales close. Housing stock changes slowly, shaped by construction activity, demolitions, conversions, and long building cycles. Structural shortage estimates sit on a longer horizon still, reflecting accumulated underbuilding over years or decades. Those measures are related, but they are not interchangeable, and treating them as if they are leads directly to bad market explanations.

This is why a market can appear to hold two contradictory conditions at once. For-sale inventory in a given metro area may have risen substantially year over year, approaching or exceeding levels not seen since before the pandemic, while the region's structural supply gap remains unchanged or continues to grow. Rising active listings do not close a structural shortage. They reflect whether current owners are choosing to sell and whether new construction is completing and reaching buyers. A year in which more homes enter the market does not erase a decade of underbuilding.

The reverse is equally true: a structural shortage does not guarantee that every listing sells quickly, at any price, to any buyer. A market can be undersupplied in the long-term structural sense and still have weak near-term transaction volume when affordability constraints have contracted the pool of buyers who can act. Structural shortage identifies a mismatch between housing stock and what the population needs. It does not override the able-demand limitation in the near term.

When a client says they read that inventory is rising and also that there is still a housing shortage, both things may be accurate. The question is which supply measure each source is describing. For-sale inventory answers a near-term question: how many homes can I choose from this month? Structural shortage answers a longer-term question: does this region have enough housing units for the people who need to live here over time? Those questions belong to different analyses, and giving a client the right answer to either one requires knowing which question they are actually asking.

Available Supply Versus Total Housing Stock

The parallel error on the supply side is treating housing stock as supply. Total housing stock describes how many homes exist in a given geography. Available supply describes how many are actively offered for purchase, in a condition buyers can acquire, at prices sellers will accept.

A neighborhood with 4,000 homes may have 18 of them for sale in a given month. The remaining 3,982 are occupied by owners who have no current motivation to sell, occupied by renters, vacant for reasons that do not include a listing, or held under conditions that make selling financially irrational. When those owners do not list, active inventory reflects their decision. Low inventory in this scenario does not signal scarcity in any absolute sense. It signals the unwillingness of current owners to sell under current conditions.

This distinction becomes most visible in periods when the lock-in effect is strongest. A homeowner with a mortgage at a rate well below current market levels has a financial disincentive to sell that goes beyond preference. Every home they might purchase as a replacement carries a higher rate and a higher monthly payment for the same property. Supply is constrained not by physical scarcity but by financial conditions that make listing irrational for a substantial share of potential sellers.

How Price Pressure Forms

When able demand exceeds available supply, buyers compete for limited options. Competition produces faster absorption, more multiple-offer situations, and prices that clear at or above original list. The pressure runs upward.

When available supply exceeds able demand, sellers compete for a limited pool of buyers who can act. Listings sit longer, price reductions become more frequent, and sellers accept offers below their original ask. The pressure runs downward.

Balance is the zone where the number of buyers who can act and the number of homes available are roughly matched, and most transactions close near asking price without urgency on either side.

The critical observation is that price pressure is a function of the relationship between these two variables, not a function of either one in isolation. A market with low supply and equally low demand may have almost no price pressure in either direction if both sides are symmetrically constrained. A market with rising supply and rising demand may still show upward price pressure if demand is growing faster than supply. The count of listings and the volume of buyer interest are inputs. Their ratio is the signal.

When Both Sides Shift at the Same Time

Supply and demand are often analyzed as if one moves while the other holds steady. In residential real estate, they frequently shift in the same direction simultaneously, and understanding both movements is what separates a market read from a market guess.

When interest rates rise sharply, able demand contracts: fewer buyers qualify for loans sufficient to purchase at prevailing prices. At the same time, the motivation of sellers with low-rate mortgages to list declines, because selling means giving up a rate they cannot replicate on a replacement home. The result can be a market where both demand and supply have contracted: fewer able buyers, fewer motivated sellers, and fewer transactions overall. This does not produce a clean buyer's market or a clean seller's market. It produces a slower, more constrained market, with neither side holding the structural advantage that a clean imbalance would create.

The reverse also occurs. When rates fall after a period of elevated levels, able demand expands as more buyers can qualify at prevailing prices, and sellers who had been waiting for better conditions return with new listings. Both sides activate, which can produce rising transaction volume without dramatic pricing pressure if the expansion is roughly symmetrical.

Why Housing Does Not Adjust Like a Liquid Market

In a liquid commodity market, prices adjust quickly when supply and demand are out of balance. If inventory exceeds demand, prices fall until buyers return. If buyers outrun supply, prices rise until some are priced out. The adjustment is visible and relatively fast.

Residential real estate does not adjust this way, and understanding why prevents a persistent category of analytical error.

Homes are not interchangeable. Every property is a unique combination of location, condition, layout, age, and neighborhood characteristics. A buyer who cannot afford the listing on one street does not seamlessly substitute the listing on another. The interchangeability that makes commodity markets liquid does not operate the same way in housing.

Sellers have an alternative to selling. In most commodity markets, producers who cannot sell at their target price face pressure to lower it or exit the market. A homeowner who cannot get the price she expects can withdraw the listing, rent the property, or simply stay. The "price falls until buyers appear" mechanism assumes sellers must sell. Many do not.

Transaction costs are high. Agent commissions, closing costs, moving expenses, and the time required to complete a transaction mean that both buyers and sellers need a meaningful expected benefit to justify moving. These friction costs slow the adjustment process and reduce the responsiveness of housing markets to short-term supply and demand signals.

Financing constraints complicate clearing. A buyer who is priced out at current rates may not return when prices fall by 5 percent if the monthly payment at those prices and those rates still exceeds their qualifying threshold. The clearing mechanism is more complicated than price alone, because affordability is a function of both price and rate simultaneously.

The practical result is that housing markets can persist in disequilibrium for months or years before adjusting, and agents who expect the fast, clean corrections that liquid markets produce will consistently misread the timing and direction of residential market movement.

Two Markets, Same Inventory

Example: Two comparable markets each show 380 active listings at the end of the month.

Market A: Mortgage rates are at 4.8 percent. At that rate, the median household income in the market qualifies for a loan sufficient to purchase at or near the median listing price. Buyers are able to act. Showing activity is strong. Average days on market for homes that sell: 14 days. The pending-to-active ratio is 38 percent. Well-priced listings attract multiple offers. Price reductions are rare.

Market B: The same active count of 380 listings. Mortgage rates have risen to 7.3 percent. At that rate, the same median household income qualifies for a loan that covers roughly $85,000 less than the median listing price. The pool of buyers able to act at current prices has contracted materially. Showing activity is lighter. Average days on market for homes that sell: 38 days. The pending-to-active ratio is 11 percent. Price reductions are common, but prices have not fallen enough to offset the rate increase for most of the buyer pool.

Market	Active Listings	Mortgage Rate	Pending-to-Active Ratio	Avg. Days on Market
Market A	380	4.8%	0.38	14 days
Market B	380	7.3%	0.11	38 days

Both markets have 380 active listings. The supply count is identical. In Market A, an active and able buyer pool is meeting that supply and transactions are clearing. In Market B, the buyer pool that can act at current prices is small relative to the available listings, and the market is producing fewer transactions without a price correction large enough to close the gap.

This is the kind of market where the usual shorthand fails in front of a client. A seller hears “low inventory” and expects leverage. A buyer hears “slow market” and expects discounts. Both may be missing the same mechanism: the supply that exists is not necessarily the supply buyers can or want to buy, and the buyers who want to purchase are not necessarily able to act at current prices and rates. The fuller analysis explains why reality feels slow even when the surface-level count looks tight.

How to Use Supply and Demand in Practice

When pricing a listing, specify the able buyer pool in the relevant segment, not just the metro-area inventory count. The supply that affects a specific listing is the active inventory in the same price range, property type, and geography competing for the same buyers. And the demand that matters is not the population of people who want to own homes in the area, but the number who are financially able to act in that segment at current prices and rates. A pricing recommendation built on metro-level supply without knowing the affordability picture of the relevant buyer pool may be right under one set of rate and income conditions and significantly wrong under another.

In seller conversations, explain why low inventory does not automatically guarantee pricing power. A seller who expects that thin supply means she can price above recent comparable sales and find a motivated buyer has understood only half of the equation. If the buyer pool at her price point is constrained by rates or income thresholds, fewer able buyers will see her listing and be in a position to make an offer, regardless of what the inventory count shows. The pricing argument requires both sides: what is the supply picture in her specific segment, and how large is the able-buyer pool that is actively searching and financially prepared to act?

In buyer conversations, explain the difference between a slow market and a buyer's market. A buyer who sees low transaction volume and concludes she has pricing leverage may be working from an incomplete picture if the affordability constraints slowing the market are also affecting her position relative to sellers. A constrained market with low volume on both sides produces fewer transactions without necessarily producing price concessions from sellers who have no urgency to sell. The leverage calculation requires knowing whether able demand is genuinely thin relative to available supply, not just whether the market feels slow.

When explaining a volume decline, distinguish between supply falling and demand falling. A market where transaction volume dropped because fewer listings entered differs from one where volume dropped because fewer buyers could act. Both produce lower sales counts. The first may produce stable or rising prices as buyers compete for fewer options. The second may produce flat or declining prices as sellers compete for a shrinking buyer pool. The explanation the data supports changes the advice you give, and the two explanations are not interchangeable.

Market Literacy Takeaway

Supply and demand explain the pressure. Available listings and able buyers are the supply and demand that actually matter. Total housing stock and desire to own are background conditions that shape the market without running it.

Use This When

- Explaining to a seller why low inventory has not produced the offer activity or pricing power she expected
- Advising a buyer who assumes a slow or low-inventory market means she has negotiating leverage, when both sides are constrained simultaneously
- Building a market explanation that needs to connect inventory levels, mortgage rates, affordability, and transaction volume in one coherent argument
- A client uses "supply and demand" as a complete explanation of market conditions, and the actual dynamics are more specific than that phrase captures
- Distinguishing between a rate-driven market contraction and a demand-driven correction when advising on pricing or offer strategy

Be Careful When

- Treating low inventory as sufficient evidence of seller advantage without confirming that able demand is present in the relevant price range and property type
- Treating high inventory as sufficient evidence of buyer advantage without checking whether sellers have realistic alternatives to selling at the price the buyer wants to offer
- Using metro-level supply and demand figures when the pricing or offer decision is specific to a segment or neighborhood where conditions may differ substantially
- Expecting housing markets to adjust quickly toward equilibrium; res-

idential real estate clears slowly because of property heterogeneity, seller optionality, and financing constraints

- Citing consumer surveys or stated homebuying intent as evidence of active demand without accounting for the affordability and financing gap between stated desire and completed transactions

Client Explanation

Supply and demand explain why prices rise when buyers compete for scarce listings and why prices fall when sellers are competing for fewer buyers. In residential real estate, the supply that matters is how many homes are actively for sale right now, not how many exist in the area. And the demand that matters is how many buyers can realistically complete a purchase at current prices and rates, not how many people would like to own a home eventually. When those two things are both limited at the same time, the market slows without producing a clear advantage for either side, and that is the kind of market where pricing and offer strategy need to be very precise.

CHAPTER 13

Months' Supply, Absorption Rate, and Market Balance

Two agents, same market report, same Thursday morning.

One reads the inventory figure, sees it is up 18 percent from the same period last year, and texts the other: "Looks like it's finally softening. Buyers are going to have more options."

The second agent pulls up the same report, runs two quick calculations, and replies: "Inventory is up, but so is sales volume. Absorption rate is actually higher than it was this time last year. The market is not softer. It is moving faster."

Both agents read the same number. One stopped there. The other asked what that number meant at the current pace of sales.

That second step is the difference between knowing how much inventory exists and knowing what that inventory means. Months' supply and absorption rate are the two tools that make that second step possible. They translate a raw count of active listings into something that actually tells you about market pressure, competition, and direction. Used together, they give you a clearer picture of where the market stands than any inventory headline can.

The Problem with Counting Listings

A count of active listings is a snapshot. It tells you how many homes are available right now, at this moment, in this market. What it does not tell you is whether that number is high or low relative to demand.

Three hundred active listings is a glut in a small mountain town. In a metro area moving 150 sales a month, that same count is only 2 months of inventory, which is tight and seller-favorable. The number is identical; its meaning depends entirely on the pace of sales.

Months' supply and absorption rate exist to solve this problem. Each formula connects the inventory count to the rate at which homes are actually selling, producing a number that carries interpretive meaning regardless of the size of the market.

Months' Supply: Inventory Measured in Time

Months' supply answers one question: if no new listings came on the market today, how many months would it take to sell everything currently available at the current sales pace?

It is a time-based measure. It converts a raw listing count into a forward-looking estimate of runway.

The formula:
Active listings / Average monthly sales = Months' supply

The "average monthly sales" figure is worth a note. Using only the prior month's closed sales makes the calculation sensitive to seasonal swings. A longer average smooths that noise and produces a more stable estimate when months' supply is being used to assess broader market conditions rather than point-in-time activity. A shorter lookback can still be useful when the market is changing quickly, but the limitation should be named.

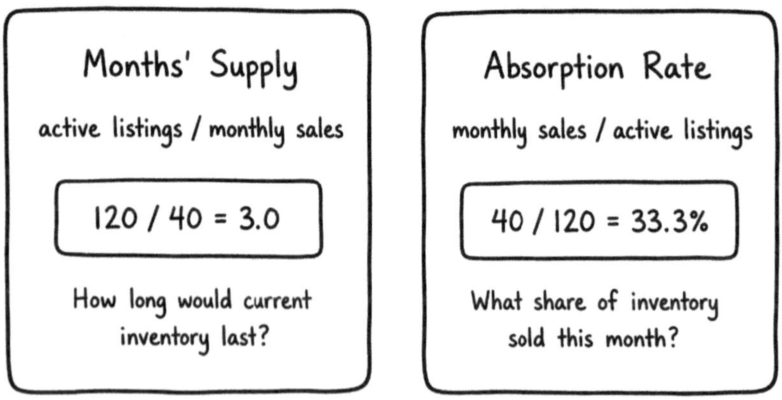

Example: A market has 120 active listings. Over the past 12 months, an average of 40 homes sold per month. Months' supply = 120 / 40 = 3.0. At the current pace, it would take 3 months to sell through all current inventory if no new listings were added.

Three months of supply usually indicates that inventory is constrained relative to the current sales pace. A higher months' supply figure generally means buyers have more options and sellers have more competition. The exact point where a market feels balanced depends on the segment, property type, price tier, season, and local norms.

Treat the familiar thresholds as orientation points, not verdicts. Three months of supply may signal pressure in one segment and normal conditions in another. If luxury condos are carrying far more inventory than entry-level homes, the blended market number is technically accurate but professionally incomplete. It tells you what the market averages. It does not tell you what your client is facing.

Absorption Rate: Inventory Measured as Pace

Absorption rate answers a slightly different question: what percentage of active inventory sold last month?

Where months' supply is time-based, absorption rate is pace-based. Months' supply says "how long is the runway." Absorption rate says "how fast are we moving down it."

The formula:
Homes sold / Active listings = Absorption rate (expressed as a percentage)

Using the same example as before: 40 homes sold / 120 active listings = 0.333, or 33.3% absorption rate. About one-third of the available supply sold during the month.

The 33.3% figure signals fast absorption, and it aligns with the 3.0 months' supply calculation. They should agree, because they are measuring the same thing.

Two Formulas, One Relationship

Months' supply and absorption rate are inverses of each other. The numerator and denominator flip. This is not a coincidence. Both formulas are describing the same underlying relationship between inventory and sales volume, just from opposite directions.

When months' supply goes down, absorption rate goes up. When months' supply is high, absorption rate is low. They move in opposite directions because they represent opposite perspectives on the same ratio.

You can also convert directly between them: absorption rate is roughly the inverse of months' supply expressed differently. A 33.3% absorption rate corresponds to approximately 3 months' supply (1 / 0.333 = 3). A 20% absorption rate corresponds to 5 months' supply (1 / 0.20 = 5). A 16.7% absorption rate corresponds to approximately 6 months' supply. The math is the point: the two numbers are not separate signals.

Understanding this relationship prevents a common error: using one metric to confirm the other as if they were independent data sources. They are not. They are the same measurement from two angles. If months' supply says seller's market and absorption rate says buyer's market, you have a calculation error, not a paradox.

The question of which metric to use depends on what the conversation requires. Months' supply is often more intuitive for clients: "there are three months of homes available" is easier to process than "33 percent of listings sold last month." Absorption rate is often more useful when comparing market velocity across time periods or explaining pace to an analytically oriented client. Both belong in a complete market read.

What These Metrics Do Not Tell You

Months' supply and absorption rate tell you where the market is right now. They do not tell you which direction it is moving.

A months' supply of 3.0 could be improving from 2.5 last quarter (supply is building, conditions easing slightly) or declining from 4.0 (supply is tightening, competition increasing). The point-in-time number reads identically in both cases. To know direction, you need to track the metric over time, which is why comparing to prior months and prior years matters more than any single reading.

Neither metric distinguishes between inventory growth that signals a structural shift and inventory growth that is seasonal. Spring brings more listings. That seasonal inventory increase can push months' supply up without any reduction in demand. An agent who reads the spring inventory surge as "the market is softening" without checking whether sales volume is also rising will draw the wrong conclusion. This is the exact error the agent in the opening made.

Neither metric tells you why the balance is what it is. Three months of supply could mean high demand with low inventory. It could also mean moderate demand with extremely low inventory. It could reflect a surge in sales that pulled down a previously higher figure. The metric is the result of a relationship, not an explanation of why that relationship exists.

The Number That Hides Three Markets

Metro-wide months' supply is useful for context and useless for positioning.

A market reporting 3.0 months of supply overall may contain three completely different realities at the price-tier level:

Example: A metro area shows 3.0 months' supply overall. Broken down by price tier: entry-level homes (under $400,000) show 1.5 months' supply. Mid-market homes ($400,000 to $700,000) show 3.0 months' supply. Luxury homes (above $700,000) show 8.0 months' supply. The entry-level segment is tight and competitive. The luxury segment gives buyers more options and sellers more competition. The composite number obscures both.

This segmentation is what the opening agents missed. The inventory report they read reflected the broader metro area. The clients they work with do not live in that metro-area composite. They live in a price range, a neighborhood, a property type. The 3.0 months' supply headline tells them almost nothing useful about how to price a listing or structure an offer.

Running months' supply and absorption rate at the segment level, not just the market level, is where these metrics earn their value.

How to Use Both in Practice

In listing presentations: Months' supply tells the seller how competitive the environment is in their price range. A seller listing at $450,000 in a 1.5-month supply segment needs to understand that if they overprice by 5 percent, they will not sit unnoticed in a field of similar homes. There are very few similar homes. The absorption rate tells you how fast the market is moving through what is available. Together, they build the case for pricing precision.

In buyer consultations: The entry-level buyer who says "there seem to be so many houses right now" may be reading the metro-area headlines.

Showing them that their actual search range has 1.5 months of supply, not 3.0, reframes the conversation. The headline inventory increase does not apply to them.

In offer strategy: When absorption is fast enough that a large share of available listings is selling each month, a buyer who asks for extensive concessions or a long inspection period is competing against buyers who are not. Months' supply and absorption rate quantify why a buyer needs to position aggressively, rather than leaving it to the agent to assert authority.

In market updates: Clients who receive monthly market emails can be given both figures with a one-sentence interpretation. "Months' supply is low in your target range, and absorption is fast compared with recent history. Both indicate competitive seller-favorable conditions, consistent with last month." That is more informative than a headline and more credible than an opinion.

The field move is to make the segment visible. A seller does not need the metro's blended number if her listing competes in a narrow price band with a different absorption pattern. A buyer does not need the market average if her search range has half the inventory and twice the velocity. The metric becomes useful when it describes the slice of the market where the client is actually making a decision.

Market Literacy Takeaway

Months' supply and absorption rate are the same ratio read two ways, not two independent signals. The metro-level number is a blended average; the segment number is what your client is actually facing.

Use This When

- Building a listing presentation that explains why pricing matters in the current supply environment
- Preparing a buyer for the level of competition in their specific price range
- Responding to a client who has seen an inventory headline and drawn the wrong conclusion

- Comparing this month's market conditions to the same period last year
- Segmenting market conditions by price tier to show how the overall number misrepresents specific sub-markets

Be Careful When

- Using a single month's absorption rate in isolation; seasonal sales volume swings can distort the figure significantly without any change in underlying demand
- Presenting metro-wide months' supply as if it applies to a specific property or price range; segment it before using it
- Calculating months' supply with a single prior month's sales figure rather than a rolling average; doing so amplifies seasonal noise
- Using months' supply and absorption rate as confirming evidence of each other; they are derived from the same inputs and will always point the same direction

Client Explanation

At the current sales pace, there are about 2 months of inventory in your price range. That means if no new homes came on the market today, what's listed now would sell through in roughly 2 months. A number that low means buyers are competing for a limited pool of homes, so a well-priced listing tends to move quickly and there's little room to test a high price. If it were closer to 6 months, you'd have more options as a buyer and more competition as a seller. Right now it's on the low end, which is what's driving the pricing approach I'm recommending.

CHAPTER 14

Mortgage Rates and Affordability

A home can carry the same price, the same down payment, and the same loan amount, yet become a meaningfully different purchase the moment the rate changes. Nothing in the listing has moved. The square footage is the same. The lot is the same. The seller is still asking the same number. What changes is the payment attached to borrowing the money, and for most financed buyers, that is where the transaction leaves the listing page and becomes a household budget question.

That contrast is easy to underestimate because housing is quoted in price while affordability is usually experienced in monthly cost. A buyer may focus on whether the purchase price stayed flat or whether a seller reduced the ask by an amount that sounds significant on paper. But if the financing environment shifted in the meantime, the relevant comparison is not just price against price. It is payment against payment. A lower price paired with a meaningfully higher rate can leave the buyer in a worse position than the higher price did at the earlier rate, not because the home changed, but because the cost of carrying the loan did.

This is why mortgage rates do not sit at the edge of the affordability conversation. They are inside it. Rates change what a given income can qualify for, what payment feels tolerable even when qualification is still technically possible, and how many buyers remain able to compete in a given price range without the sticker price moving much at all. In housing, price matters. For most buyers using financing, payment is where affordability actually gets decided.

The Payment Is the Affordability Question

A home purchase is quoted in price, but most buyers live it as a payment. The question a buyer with a $400,000 budget is actually asking is not whether they can come up with $400,000; it is whether the monthly payment attached to a loan of that size, at the current rate and their down payment, fits within their income, their debt obligations, and their willingness to commit.

This is not a subtle distinction. For most buyers, the payment is the operative variable. Lenders assess it through debt-to-income ratio (DTI), the relationship between a borrower's monthly debt obligations and gross monthly income. Exact limits vary by loan product, borrower profile, and underwriting conditions, but the mechanism is straightforward: when the rate rises on the same purchase price, the monthly payment rises, DTI rises with it, and buyers who were comfortably within qualification limits may find themselves at the edge or outside them.

This mechanism is why a rate change is a demand event, not just a cost event. It does not just make the same house more expensive to carry. It removes buyers from the market entirely.

How Rates Move the Payment

The relationship between rate and payment on a fixed-rate mortgage is not complicated, but the scale of the effect surprises many people who have not run the math.

On a 30-year fixed mortgage, a rate increase of one percentage point raises the monthly principal-and-interest payment by roughly $59 to $68 per $100,000 borrowed across common rate ranges. On a $400,000 loan, that is roughly $236 to $274 per month per one-point rate move. Across a move from 4.0 percent to 7.5 percent, the cumulative effect on the same $400,000 loan is about $887 per month.

A simple comparison illustrates the payment difference on a $500,000 purchase with a $400,000 loan at three different rate levels:

Example: A buyer is considering a $500,000 purchase with 20 percent down and a $400,000 loan. At 4.0 percent interest, the approximate monthly principal-and-interest payment is $1,910. At 6.0 percent, the same loan produces a monthly payment of approximately $2,398. At 7.5 percent, the payment rises to approximately $2,797. The purchase price has not changed.

The home has not changed. The additional $887 per month between the 4.0 and 7.5 percent scenarios is not a difference in what the home costs; it is a difference in what the financing costs. For a buyer working within a monthly payment budget, those two things are identical in practice.

Purchasing Power

The inverse of the payment calculation is purchasing power: the total loan amount a buyer can access at a given monthly budget and rate.

If a buyer can comfortably carry a principal-and-interest payment of $2,000 per month on a 30-year fixed mortgage, that budget reaches further at 4 percent than at 7 percent. At 4 percent, a $2,000 monthly P&I supports a loan of approximately $419,000. At 7 percent, the same payment supports approximately $301,000. The buyer's income has not changed. Their savings have not changed. Their stated desire to own a home has not changed. Their purchasing power has contracted by roughly $118,000 because the cost of borrowing changed.

This compression happens across the entire buyer pool simultaneously, which is why rate changes produce market-wide effects rather than affecting only buyers at the margin. When rates rise quickly and substantially, a meaningful share of the buyers who were active at the old rate level find that the price range they were shopping in has moved beyond what their payment budget can reach.

Willing Demand Versus Able Demand

Chapter 12 introduced the distinction between willing demand and able demand in the context of supply-and-demand mechanics. Mortgage rates are one of the primary mechanisms by which that gap widens or narrows.

Willing demand for homeownership is structurally large and more stable than the pool of buyers who can act at any given rate and price. Stated intent does not represent active demand; it represents aspiration. Active demand is the pool of buyers who are willing, financially qualified, and prepared to close a transaction at current prices and rates.

When rates rise quickly, the able pool contracts. A buyer who was pre-approved at a comfortable payment level three months ago may be at or past their qualification ceiling today at the same price. A buyer who was looking comfortably in the $550,000 to $600,000 range may need to revise their ceiling to $480,000 to stay within their payment comfort. The desire to own has not changed. The financial capacity to act, at a specific price in a specific market, has.

This is the mechanism behind declining transaction volume in rising-rate environments. It is not that buyers stop wanting homes. It is that the pool of buyers who can write a competitive, qualifying offer at current prices at current rates becomes smaller.

How Higher Rates Slow Demand Without Automatically Lowering Prices

A common inference about rising rates is that they cause home prices to fall. The relationship exists but is not automatic, and understanding why it is not one-to-one is important for advising both buyers and sellers accurately.

Higher rates reduce able demand. Fewer buyers can qualify and compete at any given price. For a price to fall, sellers must be willing to accept less, and many sellers, particularly those who do not need to sell, are not. A seller with no financial urgency and no competing offer may simply withdraw from the market rather than accept a price that does not meet their expectation. That choice protects their price and removes a listing from the active count, which tightens supply and provides some counterweight to the demand compression.

The result is not price collapse; it is reduced transaction volume. Fewer homes are listed. Fewer buyers are competing. The matches that do occur happen at prices that may be flat or modestly lower, not at dramatically lower prices. Days on market lengthen. Price reductions become more common at the listing level, because individual sellers overprice into a buyer pool that is smaller than it appears. But the market-wide median may hold, because the transactions that do close are still clearing at prices buyers and sellers can agree on.

This is why price stability and market stability are not the same thing in a rising-rate environment. Volume can fall, pace can slow, and negotiation dynamics can shift substantially in buyers' favor without the median closing price showing a dramatic move.

How Rates Affect Different Buyer Types Differently

Rate sensitivity is not uniform across the buyer pool, and treating it as such misses important differences in how a rate move lands depending on where in the market a buyer is positioned.

Entry-level buyers tend to be the most payment-sensitive. They are often purchasing with smaller down payments, which means larger loans relative to purchase price. They frequently have less financial cushion to absorb a higher monthly payment. Their debt-to-income ratios are typically tighter, which means a modest payment increase can push them outside qualification at their target price range. When rates rise, entry-level buyers feel the compression first and most acutely.

Move-up buyers with substantial equity carry more flexibility. A seller who captured significant appreciation over several years of ownership may be bringing a large down payment to the next purchase, which reduces the loan size and, with it, the payment sensitivity to rate moves. Their payment calculus is still affected by rates, but the effect is smaller relative to the transaction size.

Cash buyers are not affected at all. In markets where a meaningful share of transactions are all-cash, particularly at higher price points, a rate change may alter the competitive dynamics less than the headline number suggests. Investors, second-home buyers, and buyers in high-equity situations can insulate themselves from rate changes in ways that first-time, entry-level buyers cannot.

Understanding which segment of the buyer pool is most relevant to a specific listing or a specific client's situation is the practical application of this: rate changes do not flatten the market uniformly. They compress specific segments and leave others relatively unaffected.

The Seller Side: Rate Lock-In and Supply Contraction

Mortgage rates do not only affect buyers. They affect the supply side of the market in a way that compounds the demand effect rather than offsetting it.

Homeowners who purchased or refinanced during lower-rate periods may be holding mortgages at rates well below what is available in a higher-rate environment. Selling the home and buying another requires giving up that rate. Even if the seller can find a comparable replacement property at the same price, the monthly payment on a new mortgage at market rates is meaningfully higher. For many owners, the math does not favor moving, and so they do not list.

In 2023, this was described *ad nauseam* as "golden handcuffs." The phrase got tired because it was everywhere, but it pointed to a legitimate constraint: a homeowner's existing mortgage rate had become valuable enough that selling meant giving up a financial advantage.

This dynamic, commonly called the rate lock-in effect, constrains supply at the same time that demand is contracting. In theory, less demand and less supply could produce a stable price level, which is part of why prices can hold even as transaction volume falls. In practice, the composition of what does list shifts: sellers with financial urgency or life circumstances that override the financial disincentive enter the market, while owners who would otherwise be move-up or move-down sellers stay in place.

The resulting market has less of everything. Fewer listings. Fewer active buyers. Fewer transactions. The homes that do sell often take longer and face more scrutiny, because the qualified buyer pool is smaller and less willing to stretch.

Reading Rates Alongside Other Indicators

Mortgage rates are one variable in a multi-factor affordability picture. They interact with income levels, home prices, available inventory, down payment requirements, and local market dynamics in ways that make rate-only analysis incomplete.

A rate increase in a market with rapidly rising incomes is less constraining than the same rate increase in a market where incomes are flat. A rate decrease in a market with severely constrained inventory may not produce the buyer surge it would in a market with ample supply. The payment calculation tells you what the monthly cost is; it does not tell you whether buyers have the income to support it, the down payment to access it, or the confidence to commit to it.

Affordability should be read alongside DOM, price reduction frequency, pending-to-active ratios, and concession trends in closed transactions. The combination of those indicators tells a cleaner story than rates alone.

How to Use Rate and Affordability Analysis in Practice

In buyer consultations: Frame the conversation around payment range before discussing price range. A buyer who knows they are looking for a home where the monthly P&I falls below a specific number is better positioned to understand why their effective price ceiling shifts with rates. Before any showing, confirm whether the pre-approval is current; a pre-approval from three months ago at a rate that has since moved meaningfully is not the same instrument it was.

In seller pricing conversations: When rates are elevated, the buyer pool qualified to purchase at a given price is smaller than it was at lower rates. This does not mean the price needs to drop by the full affordability compression amount. It does mean that pricing to the market requires understanding who is in the market, at what payment they can act, and at what price the pool of able buyers begins to thin. A seller pricing above what the able buyer pool can support in a higher-rate environment will see it in DOM, not immediately in offers.

In negotiation: Rate buydowns, where a seller contributes funds toward buying down the buyer's rate for the first years of the loan, can be a more effective concession structure than an equivalent price reduction in certain buyer profiles. The mechanics matter and should be run through a lender, but the principle is that payment-sensitive buyers may respond more directly to a lower rate than to a lower price, because the payment difference compounds across 12 months rather than appearing once in the purchase number.

In market reports: When reporting on market conditions in a period of rate movement, present both the price trend and the affordability trend. A market where prices have held flat while rates have risen by two points has become less affordable even though the comps show stability. Naming that distinction is what separates a market report from a statistic.

The field version of this is often blunt. A buyer comes back to the same price range after rates move and feels as if the market has not changed because the listings look familiar. The payment says otherwise. A seller sees stable closed comps and assumes demand should still be there. The showing traffic says otherwise. Putting the payment reality in front of the client changes the conversation from "prices are up or down" to "who can actually act at this number now?"

Market Literacy Takeaway

Mortgage rates do not directly set home values, but they change the monthly payment attached to a price. For buyers purchasing with financing, that payment is where affordability lives. A market with prices holding flat but rates rising is not the same market it was when rates were lower, and treating it as such understates how much the buyer pool has actually contracted.

Use This When

- A buyer is pre-approved and shopping near the top of their payment range, and rates have moved since the approval
- A seller asks why buyer activity has slowed even though recent closed comps haven't shown price declines
- A buyer returns to a listing after an absence and expects the reduced price to mean better affordability, without accounting for rate movement in the interval
- Explaining to a client why transaction volume can fall without a corresponding drop in median price
- Advising a buyer in an entry-level price range where payment sensitivity to rate changes is highest
- A seller is considering whether to offer a rate buydown as a concession versus a price reduction

Be Careful When

- Claiming that rising rates directly and reliably cause home prices to fall; the relationship exists but is not automatic, and depends on seller motivation, inventory levels, and how much of the market operates with cash or high equity

- Presenting payment calculations as exact rather than approximate; mortgage math is sensitive to inputs, and any specific payment figure should be verified against a standard amortization formula before being used in a client-facing conversation
- Treating all buyers as equally rate-sensitive; cash buyers, high-equity move-up buyers, and investors are affected differently than entry-level, payment-constrained buyers
- Using a rate buydown recommendation without first running the numbers with a lender; the structure and cost vary by loan type, lender, and market conditions
- Overstating the rate lock-in effect without sourced data; the general principle is well-supported, but specific estimates of how many homeowners are locked in require a verified source before being cited to a client

Client Explanation

The home's listing price tells you what the seller is asking; the mortgage rate tells you what it costs you to borrow the money to pay that price. When rates go up, your monthly payment goes up on the same purchase even if the price hasn't moved. For most buyers, that payment is the actual budget question, not the sticker price. If rates have risen since you were last pre-approved, we should run updated numbers with your lender before we start scheduling showings, because the payment math may have shifted your effective price range even if the homes you are looking at haven't changed.

CHAPTER 15

The Fed and the Housing Market

"The Fed cut rates."

Those four words are usually delivered as if they explain far more than they do. In housing commentary, the phrase often carries an implied second sentence that never gets spoken out loud: mortgage rates should fall, buyers should come back, affordability should improve, and the market should respond. That reading is understandable, because the shorthand sounds direct. It also compresses a long chain of financial transmission into one apparently simple cause-and-effect story.

The Fed does matter to housing, but not because it pulls a direct lever on 30-year mortgage rates or home prices. A Fed decision has to work through expectations, bond markets, Treasury yields, mortgage-backed securities, lender pricing, mortgage rates, buyer payments, able demand, seller behavior, and transaction volume before it becomes a housing-market condition. Sometimes parts of that chain move quickly. Sometimes they barely move at all. Sometimes the market adjusted weeks earlier because the decision was already expected.

That is where Fed news becomes dangerous in a client conversation. The phrase "the Fed cut rates" sounds like an answer when it is really the beginning of a more complicated explanation. If you are going to use Fed news in a market conversation, you need to know which rate actually changed, which rates did not, and how a monetary-policy signal becomes, or fails to become, something a buyer or seller can feel in the market.

What the Federal Reserve Does

The Federal Reserve is the central bank of the United States. Its core responsibilities include managing monetary policy, supporting a stable financial system, and supervising certain banking institutions. In the context that matters most for housing, the Fed's primary monetary policy tool is the federal funds rate, a short-term overnight rate on transactions where banks and other eligible institutions borrow and lend balances held at the Federal Reserve.

The Fed sets a target range for this rate through the Federal Open Market Committee (FOMC), which meets regularly and issues statements about its current policy stance. The FOMC's decisions reflect the Fed's dual mandate: supporting maximum employment and stable prices. In practice, the FOMC frames price stability around 2 percent inflation over the longer run.

When the news says "the Fed raised rates" or "the Fed cut rates by half a point," that is referring to this overnight benchmark. It is the rate at which large financial institutions settle short-term balances with each other, not the rate at which a buyer in Denver or Houston closes a purchase.

What the Federal Funds Rate Is Not

The federal funds rate is a short-term overnight rate. A 30-year fixed mortgage is a long-term consumer lending product. They are not the same instrument, they do not respond to the same forces, and they do not move in lockstep.

This distinction matters because every client conversation that assumes "the Fed cut rates, so my mortgage rate will drop" is conflating two different things. The Fed sets what banks charge each other for reserves they hold overnight. A mortgage lender offers what a borrower will pay for a 30-year commitment. The factors driving those two numbers overlap, but they are not the same, and the connection between them is indirect rather than mechanical.

Where Mortgage Rates Actually Come From

To understand why the fed funds rate and mortgage rates can move in different directions, it helps to understand how mortgage rates are set.

When a lender makes a mortgage loan, it often does not hold that loan on its own books indefinitely. Many loans move through the secondary market, where mortgages are pooled, securitized, and sold to investors as

How the Fed influences housing indirectly

1. Fed policy stance

- Raises, cuts, or holds the fed funds target.
- Signals priorities on inflation, jobs, and credit.
- It does not set mortgage rates directly.

2. Short-term rates

- Overnight funding costs move first.
- Bank and money-market rates adjust quickly.
- Credit conditions begin to tighten or loosen.

3. Market expectations

- Investors price what they think comes next.
- Expected inflation, growth, and future Fed moves matter.
- Surprises can move markets before announcements.

4. Treasury yields and MBS pricing

- Long-term yields respond to expectations.
- Mortgage-backed securities reprice as spreads move.
- Lenders use this market as the starting point.

5. Mortgage rates

- Lenders translate market pricing into borrower rates.
- The move is indirect, not point-for-point.
- Borrower cost changes here.

6. Payment and affordability

- The same home price can carry a different payment.
- Qualification limits and comfort ranges shift.
- Affordability changes before prices necessarily do.

7. Able demand

- Some buyers can act; others pause.
- It varies by income, price tier, cash, and loan type.
- Pressure shows first near the payment limit.

8. Housing activity and pricing pressure

- Showings, offers, and seller behavior adjust.
- Volume often changes before closed prices do.
- Prices respond after the chain works through.

mortgage-backed securities (MBS). Investors who buy these securities require a yield, a return for committing capital to that credit risk over a long time horizon. The yield investors demand on MBS helps shape what rate lenders can offer borrowers, because the lender needs to be able to sell the loan at a price that reflects market rates.

MBS yields are influenced by many of the same forces that drive other long-term bonds. Inflation expectations matter enormously: if investors believe that inflation will be higher over the coming decade, they demand higher yields to preserve the real value of their return. Treasury yields matter, particularly the 10-year Treasury yield, because mortgage rates tend to move with long-term Treasury yields even though the two do not move in lockstep. The spread between 10-year Treasuries and 30-year mortgage rates reflects credit risk, prepayment risk, and the relative demand for mortgage credit as an investment class.

The federal funds rate, in contrast, most directly influences very short-term lending: overnight borrowing, short-term commercial credit, adjustable-rate products whose indexes are tied to shorter benchmarks. The long end of the yield curve, where mortgage pricing lives, responds to its own set of forces.

The Indirect Path

With that foundation, the connection between Fed policy and housing becomes clearer, even as it becomes less mechanical.

When the Fed tightens monetary policy by raising the federal funds rate, it is signaling an intent to cool economic activity, reduce inflation, or both. That signal reaches the bond market partly through direct effects on short-term rates and partly through expectations about future inflation and future Fed decisions. If tighter Fed policy is expected to bring inflation down, long-term inflation expectations may fall, which tends to reduce long-term bond yields. Lower long-term yields, if they materialize, can eventually translate to lower mortgage rates. If the tightening cycle is aggressive and the economy slows significantly, credit conditions may tighten across the board, affecting the spread between Treasuries and MBS.

When the Fed eases monetary policy, the same chain runs in reverse, but with the same lag, noise, and complexity at each step.

The key word throughout is "can." None of these links is guaranteed in magnitude, timing, or direction. The Fed shapes the environment; it does not control each outcome within it.

Why Announcements Do Not Translate Mechanically

The gap between Fed announcements and mortgage-rate movements is often larger than clients expect, for a reason that is fundamental to how financial markets work: markets anticipate.

Financial markets trade on expectations, not just announcements. Professional investors and institutions in the bond market monitor economic data, FOMC communications, and policy signals to estimate what the Fed is likely to do before it does it. When a rate cut is widely expected, bond yields and MBS yields may adjust before the official announcement. By the time the FOMC votes, the mortgage market may already reflect much of what clients are hearing as breaking news.

This is why a buyer who waits for a Fed announcement to move mortgage rates may be waiting for something that already happened, or waiting for a decision the market has already absorbed. The announcement is news to the public. To bond-market participants who had been watching economic data and Fed communications for months, it may be exactly what they expected.

How Fed Policy Still Matters for Housing

None of this means the Fed is irrelevant to housing. Over longer time horizons, Fed policy shapes the financial environment in ways that reach housing market conditions through multiple channels.

When the Fed maintains low rates for extended periods, as it did through much of the post-2008 recovery, the low-rate environment eventually works through bond markets and into long-term yields. Mortgage rates fall over time as that environment takes hold. Affordability improves for payment-sensitive buyers. The pool of able buyers expands. Demand increases. Transaction volume rises. Pricing pressure builds in inventory-constrained markets. The effect accumulates over months and years rather than arriving on the day of an FOMC decision.

When the Fed tightens aggressively over a short period, bond markets can adjust rapidly because expectations change sharply. Mortgage rates can move substantially, not because the fed funds rate is the same thing as a mortgage rate, but because the entire long-term rate environment reprices based on where investors expect inflation, economic growth, and Fed policy to go.

The Fed also has additional tools that can affect longer-term rates and mortgage-backed securities markets. Large-scale asset purchase programs have included Treasury securities and agency MBS, and larger Fed holdings can put downward pressure on MBS yields and mortgage rates, though the size and timing of that effect are difficult to pin down. Quantitative tightening, the reverse process, can apply upward pressure on yields by reducing that support. These tools give the Fed a more direct channel into longer-term rates than the federal funds rate alone provides, but even there the effect is not a simple one-for-one move.

The Seller Side

The Fed's influence on housing does not run only through buyer demand and mortgage rates. It also affects seller behavior, though through a different mechanism.

Sellers who hold existing mortgages at rates established when the Fed's policy environment produced lower long-term yields face a financial disincentive to sell and re-enter the market at current rates, even if they would otherwise be inclined to move. This is the rate lock-in effect described in the prior chapter, and it is partly a product of the Fed's policy history. A period of sustained low rates followed by rapid tightening can leave many homeowners reluctant to give up their existing mortgage, constraining supply at the same time that demand contracts. The result is a market where both sides can be diminished: fewer listings, fewer qualifying buyers, and lower transaction volume even without a dramatic move in median price.

A Hypothetical Case

A buyer has been watching a market for three months, waiting for the right moment. She has been following Fed communications and believes that when the Fed cuts its overnight rate, mortgage rates will fall meaningfully and she will get a better deal. The FOMC meets and votes to cut by a quarter point. She checks mortgage rates that afternoon. They have moved by less than a tenth of a percent. Her lender explains that the bond market had anticipated the cut for weeks, that 10-year Treasury yields barely shifted on the day, and that the rate she can lock today is almost identical to what she could have locked two weeks ago. The buyer delayed a decision for months waiting for an event that the mortgage market had already priced in. The Fed cut. Mortgage rates did not follow in the way she expected.

The lesson is not that Fed cuts are meaningless. It is that the announcement and the mortgage-rate outcome are not the same event. The outcome depends on what was already priced in, how bond markets responded over the preceding weeks, and whether longer-term inflation expectations actually shifted.

Common Assumption	Better Interpretation
Fed cut means mortgage rates fall immediately.	Markets may have priced in the move before the announcement.
Fed hike means prices must fall.	Affordability changes first; prices depend on supply and demand.
Fed news tells buyers what to do.	The client decision depends on payment, options, and timing.
"Wait for the next Fed cut."	A lower rate can arrive with different prices and competition.

How Agents Should Use Fed-Related News

Fed announcements create client questions that deserve accurate answers, not vague reassurances and not detailed macroeconomic lectures. The goal is to give clients enough framework to interpret what they are hearing without either inflating their expectations or dismissing a piece of news that genuinely matters over time.

The practical position for an agent: Fed news is context, not a prediction tool. When a client cites a Fed decision as a reason to act or wait, the right response is to acknowledge that the Fed matters while redirecting to what actually determines the buyer's or seller's situation: the current mortgage rate the lender is quoting, what that rate produces as a monthly payment relative to the buyer's budget, what inventory and competition look like in their specific segment, and what their own timeline and motivation require.

When mortgage rates are moving in a way that appears connected to Fed expectations, that is worth noting in a market update: "Rates have been adjusting over the past few weeks as the market has priced in an expected Fed move. Here is where rates stand today and what that means for the payment on homes in your range." That is more useful than "the Fed cut rates so this is a good time to buy."

When mortgage rates are not moving after a widely covered Fed decision, the explanation that serves clients best is also the honest one: the announcement did what markets expected, and the market had already moved.

In practice, the cleanest answer often starts with the rate sheet, not the headline. "The Fed decision matters, but your lender's quote is the number that affects your payment. Let's look at what changed there first." That keeps the conversation grounded in the client's decision instead of letting a national headline take over the room.

Market Literacy Takeaway

The Fed does not set the housing market. It changes the financial weather the housing market moves through. A Fed announcement is the start of a long chain of market adjustments, not the end of one. What matters for a buyer's payment or a seller's timing is not what the FOMC voted to do but what mortgage rates, inventory, and local market conditions are actually doing in response to the broader financial environment the Fed has shaped.

Use This When

- A buyer says they are waiting for a Fed cut before making an offer, assuming mortgage rates will drop on the day of the announcement
- A seller asks whether a rate hike means their home's value will decline
- Preparing a market update that explains why mortgage rates have not moved after a high-profile Fed announcement
- A client or colleague conflates the federal funds rate with a 30-year mortgage rate
- Explaining why the housing market can remain active during a Fed tightening period, or sluggish during an easing period, when local inventory and other conditions dominate the short-term picture
- Any conversation where a client is making a housing decision primarily based on Fed news rather than current lender quotes and local market data

Be Careful When

- Claiming that Fed cuts directly and reliably produce mortgage-rate cuts of equal size; the relationship exists but is indirect and depends on what was already priced into bond markets
- Suggesting the Fed is irrelevant; its policy stance shapes the financial

environment over time and affects borrowing costs, affordability, and market activity

- Making specific claims about historical mortgage-rate or fed-funds-rate levels, spreads, or timelines without checking the underlying data first
- Overpromising to clients: "rates will come down when the Fed cuts" is not a promise an agent can make
- Presenting the indirect-path chain as a precise causal model; it captures the general direction but markets add noise, lag, and divergence at every step

Client Explanation

When the Fed changes its overnight rate, mortgage rates do not automatically follow by the same amount or on the same day, because mortgage rates respond to long-term bond markets rather than to the Fed's short-term target. Often, if a rate move is expected, the bond market has already adjusted before the announcement, and mortgage rates may have moved weeks earlier or may barely move when the news breaks. The most useful number for your decision is not what the Fed announced but what rate your lender is quoting today and what payment that produces at your budget. That is the number that determines whether the deal works, not the headline from the FOMC meeting.

CHAPTER 16

New Construction Signals

The seller knows about the builder community down the road. They've seen the sales trailer open on weekends, and they want to know whether those new homes change what their own property can command.

The answer is that they might, but only if the construction has become part of the buyer's actual choice set. A permit pulled months ago may be useful context, and a project still behind a fence may matter later. Neither carries the same force as a finished home nearby that buyers can tour today, especially if the builder is using incentives to make the payment look better than a resale alternative.

Those signals have to be separated. New construction data describes a pipeline, and each stage has a different meaning for a buyer or seller decision. The useful question is not simply whether building is happening. It is whether that building has become market pressure for the specific property in front of you.

What New Construction Data Measures

When real estate professionals talk about new construction data, they typically mean the monthly figures published through the U.S. Census Bureau's New Residential Construction program, based on building permit data and the Survey of Construction, which is partially funded by the U.S. Department of Housing and Urban Development. Those releases separate residential construction activity into distinct stages: units authorized by permit, units authorized but not started, units started, units under construction, and units completed.

Each stage measures something different.

Building permits are authorizations issued by local governments for new residential construction. A permit means that a builder has received approval to build. It does not mean that ground has been broken, that a home is coming soon, or that any unit is available for purchase. Permits are the furthest upstream point in the pipeline. They signal intended future supply, sometimes months or years before anything is deliverable.

Housing starts occur when construction begins on a new residential unit, generally counted when excavation begins for the footings or foundation. A start confirms that a permitted project has moved to action, but the home does not yet exist in any livable form.

Homes under construction represent units where work is actively ongoing between the start and the completion. This figure captures the full backlog of units being built at any given moment. It is not a count of homes available to buyers; rather, it is a count of homes in progress.

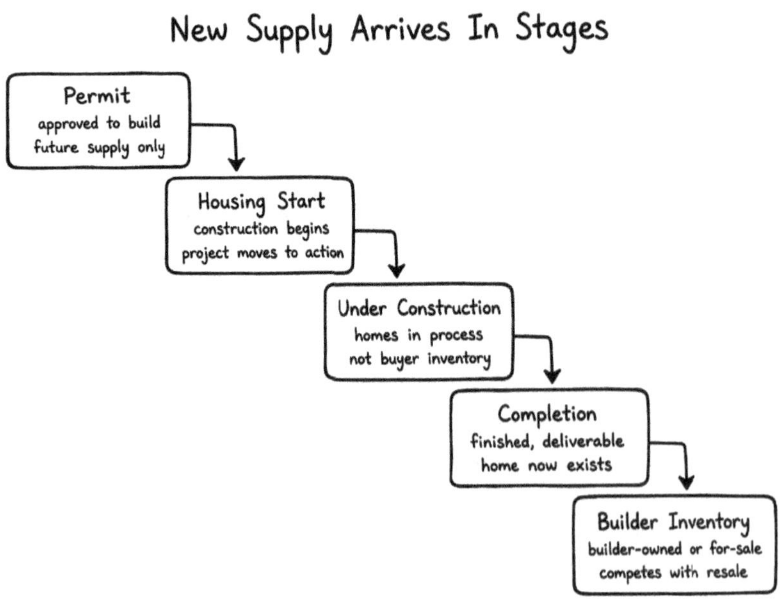

Completions occur when a residential unit reaches the finished end of the construction process. Census completion rules are tied to finished flooring and occupancy or availability for occupancy, depending on property type. For market-reading purposes, a completion is the first point in the pipeline where the home exists as a deliverable product. By the time a completion is recorded, the permit was pulled well before today's market conversation.

Builder inventory refers to completed homes that a builder owns and has not yet sold, as well as homes under construction that are available for purchase before completion. Builder inventory is the stage at which a new-construction home is directly comparable to resale listings.

What the Pipeline Means for Market Analysis

Because each stage sits at a different distance from actual buyer availability, each tells a different story about the market's forward-looking condition.

Permits are the leading indicator. A surge in permit issuance tells you that builders are betting on future demand. It does not tell you that supply is arriving now, or even soon. The lag from permit to completion can run many months and sometimes longer, depending on construction type, labor and material availability, financing conditions, inspection schedules, and local permitting processes. Attached and multifamily projects often follow different timelines.

Starts confirm that intention has moved to action. A high starts figure means the forward supply pipeline is filling, but the units are not yet available to buyers. Watching starts relative to completions tells you whether the pipeline is converting at a steady rate or whether a backlog is building.

Completions are the lagging indicator. They reflect past builder confidence, past demand projections, and past financing and land decisions. A completions surge today is the result of starts decisions made well before current market conditions existed. Completions tell you where the pipeline is arriving, not where it is going.

Builder inventory, particularly completed standing inventory, is the figure most directly comparable to resale listings. When builders hold unsold finished homes, they carry those costs until a sale closes. That carrying cost creates incentive to move units, and that incentive often produces the competitive tools that make new construction most visible in a resale seller's market.

What New Construction Data Does Not Tell You

Two gaps matter most when reading new construction figures.

The segmentation problem. Metro-level new construction data is an aggregate. It blends single-family detached homes in the outer suburbs, attached townhomes near employment centers, and high-rise multifamily in urban cores, across every price point and geography in the metro area. A headline that says construction starts rose in any given metro area does not tell you whether those units are in the price tier, product type, or geography that is relevant to your client's situation.

A buyer looking for an attached townhome priced between $500,000 and $600,000 in a specific corridor is not interchangeable with that metro-area total. If attached homes in their target area are delivering at a rate that exceeds buyer demand for that product, they are in a soft buyer condition within a metro area that overall looks tight. If the metro area's construction growth is concentrated in single-family homes priced above $750,000, the segment they need may remain undersupplied regardless of what the headline says.

The structural shortage vs. submarket competition distinction. A regional or national housing supply deficit does not preclude localized builder delivery surges in specific product types or corridors. Both conditions can exist simultaneously. A metro area with a long-term structural housing supply gap can still have a three-block corridor where four new attached-home communities are delivering units in the same six-month window.

For a resale seller whose property competes directly with that corridor's new inventory, the structural shortage exists but it is not the relevant fact for today's pricing conversation. The four sales offices open within a mile are the relevant fact.

When Builders Compete Directly With Resale

The point where new construction most directly affects an active resale listing is when builder inventory enters the buyer's comparison set.

A buyer considering a resale townhome will often tour new-build alternatives in the same corridor at comparable price points. That comparison may seem straightforward until you account for what builders can offer that resale sellers typically cannot.

Large-volume builders may carry financing relationships, margin structures, and inventory pressures that allow them to offer buyers tools resale sellers cannot match directly. Incentive availability, type, and magnitude vary by builder, project, lender relationship, and market conditions, but the toolkit can include:

- **Rate buydowns:** a builder or its affiliated lender pays to reduce the buyer's interest rate temporarily or for the full loan term, reducing the effective monthly payment relative to a resale alternative at a similar purchase price
- **Closing-cost credits:** cash contributions toward buyer closing costs, reducing out-of-pocket requirements at close
- **Design and upgrade packages:** fixtures, flooring, appliances, or finishes included at no additional cost that a resale home cannot add without a price reduction
- **Agent bonus programs:** additional compensation offered for a closed transaction in the community, subject to disclosure, brokerage policy, and local rules
- **Warranty coverage:** new-build structural and mechanical system warranties that resale homes cannot offer without separate third-party purchase

When a builder is holding completed standing inventory, the motivation to offer incentives can increase. Finished, unsold homes tie up capital and create pressure to convert inventory into closed sales. The incentive packages are not always prominently advertised at the top-level price point; buyers touring a builder community may be offered a buydown or credit not listed on the initial price sheet.

This does not mean new builds are always the better deal for a buyer. Resale homes in established neighborhoods may offer location, lot size, school boundary, or community maturity that a new-build corridor cannot. But for a resale seller, the question is not whether new construction is generally preferable. The question is whether it is sufficiently competitive at a given moment, in a given corridor, to affect buyer behavior and buyer willingness to pay the resale price.

A Hypothetical Case

A resale townhome seller in a suburban corridor is preparing to list at $575,000. Two months before she lists, three new attached-home communities in the same corridor begin delivering completed units. Each builder is offering a two-year rate buydown through its preferred lender and a $10,000 closing-cost credit on select homes. The builder homes range from $560,000 to $595,000 and carry full new-build warranties. A buyer touring the resale home tours two builder models the same afternoon. The resale home is a 2019 build in good condition, but it cannot offer a rate buydown or a builder warranty. The broader metro area has a structural housing shortage at the aggregate level. That is an accurate fact. It does not change the pricing calculation for this seller. The relevant competition is not the broader metro-area deficit. It is the three sales offices open within a mile. Her agent advises a pricing and preparation strategy that accounts for what buyers will compare, not just what the comps say on paper.

How Agents Should Use New Construction Data

New construction signals are most useful when read as forward-looking inputs, not current-market scorecards. The stage of the data matters as much as the number itself.

For buyer clients: A permit surge in a specific submarket means that supply may arrive months later rather than right now. A buyer with flexibility may find more choice and more builder incentive motivation if they can wait for delivery. A buyer who cannot wait may be transacting at the front end of a delivery wave, before builder competition reaches full intensity.

For resale seller clients: Completions and builder inventory figures in the seller's specific corridor are more relevant than metro-area permit totals. The question is not whether the broader metro area is building. The question is whether completed builder inventory in the seller's product type and geography is actively entering the buyer's comparison set, and whether that inventory is backed by buyer incentives the resale listing cannot match.

For price analysis: When new-build comps appear in or near a resale seller's neighborhood, they introduce an alternative pricing anchor. Buyers will compare. An agent who does not account for that comparison in pricing and marketing strategy is setting the seller up for surprise.

For market updates: Separating the pipeline stages helps clients understand what "construction is up" actually means in practice. An increase in permits means builders expect future demand. An increase in completions means past bets are now arriving as inventory. Telling clients which stage is moving, and in which segment, is more useful than reporting a headline figure without context.

The useful move before a listing appointment is to map the buyer's real alternatives. If the competing new-build community has quick move-ins, ask what incentives are actually being offered, not just what the published prices say. If the nearby construction is still upstream in the pipeline, explain that too. A crane and a completed, incentivized inventory home are both new construction signals, but they are not the same signal for a seller deciding how to price this week.

Market Literacy Takeaway

New construction data is not a current-supply number. It is a pipeline of signals at different stages. A permit surge means builders are betting on future demand; a completions surge means past bets are now arriving as inventory; builder inventory means competition open for tours today, often with rate buydowns and warranty coverage a resale seller cannot match. Reading those stages separately, segmented by product type and geography, is what tells a resale seller whether nearby construction is a distant signal or a direct threat to their price.

Use This When

- A seller asks whether new construction in the area will affect their price or sale timeline
- A buyer wants to understand how to compare a new-build with a resale option, particularly when builder incentives are in play
- Preparing a market update that includes a permit or construction-starts figure
- A client cites rising permit numbers as evidence that prices should come down soon
- A listing falls in a corridor where builder communities are delivering inventory simultaneously
- A buyer is weighing whether to wait for new construction to arrive or to act before it does

Be Careful When

- Citing metro-level construction data as though it applies uniformly to a specific price tier or geography; new construction is segmented by product type, price band, and location
- Claiming that a structural housing shortage means new construction competition is irrelevant to a specific resale seller; submarket competition can exist even in a supply-constrained metro area
- Making specific claims about builder margin flexibility or incentive capacity without checking the actual builder, lender relationship, project stage, and inventory pressure
- Presenting permits as equivalent to supply; they are the beginning of a pipeline, not the end of one
- Treating new-build and resale comparables as equivalent in a pricing analysis without accounting for the builder toolkit

Client Explanation

When you hear that permits are up or that there is a lot of building going on, that tells you what builders are planning, not what buyers can purchase today. A permit is an approval to build. It becomes a home available to buy only after construction is complete, which can take many months and sometimes longer. What matters for your situation is whether completed new-build homes in your specific area and price range are competing with what you are buying or selling. If they are, the comparison is not just about price. Builders can offer rate buydowns, warranty coverage, and design packages that a resale home cannot include. That is the competition to understand, not the metro-level headline.

CHAPTER 17

Residential Investment Metrics

Investment analysis begins by changing the question. For an owner-occupant, value is tied to use: whether the home fits the way someone wants to live. For an investor, the property has to be translated into rent, expenses, financing, risk, and expected return. A home can be appealing in the first sense and weak in the second, or plain as a place to live and still work as an investment.

That distinction matters because the same address can produce two different valuations. The owner-occupant is judging usefulness and fit. The investor is judging the relationship between price and income over time. When those questions get blended together, the analysis gets muddy quickly.

The metrics behind that second question are what separate an investor's reasoning from an owner-occupant's. Gross rent, operating expenses, NOI, cap rate, cash flow, and cash-on-cash return are not interchangeable labels for whether a property works as an investment. Each one answers a narrower question, and each one can mislead when it is used outside its proper place.

Why Investment Value Is Different From Owner-Occupant Value

When an owner-occupant evaluates a home, the value equation includes things that resist precise quantification: a layout that works for a specific family, proximity to a school or a job, the feel of a neighborhood at 7 a.m., the afternoon light in the kitchen. These factors matter. They influence price and drive buyer behavior. They are also not transferable, because the next buyer arrives with a different family, a different commute, and a different set of preferences.

An investor evaluating the same property runs a different calculation. The finishes matter only insofar as they affect rent, vacancy, or long-term maintenance cost. The school boundary matters only if it shapes the quality and stability of the tenant pool. The emotional register of the neighborhood matters only if it influences how reliably the property will attract and retain tenants.

What drives the investor's analysis is a different set of relationships: between purchase price, gross rent, operating expenses, vacancy, financing cost, expected appreciation, and required return. Those relationships are what this chapter covers.

Investment Income Statement: Order of Operations

Sign	Line item	What changes at this step	Role in analysis
+	Gross rent	• Rent at full occupancy	Top line
-	Vacancy / collection loss	• Expected rent not collected	Deduction
=	Effective gross income	• Income available before expenses	Subtotal
-	Operating expenses	• Taxes, insurance, management, repairs, reserves	Deduction
=	Net operating income (NOI)	• Operating performance before financing	Cap rate input
-	Debt service	• Loan payments	Financing enters here
=	Cash flow	• Cash left after operations and debt	Before tax
÷	Total cash invested	• Down payment, closing costs, initial capital	Investor cash
=	Cash-on-cash return	• Annual cash flow as a share of cash invested	Return metric

Gross Rent

Gross rent is the total rental income a property could produce if fully occupied for an entire year. A property that rents for $2,400 per month has a gross annual rent of $28,800.

Gross rent is the starting point for investment analysis. It is not income.

The distinction matters because a buyer who evaluates a rental property on gross rent alone is treating an optimistic ceiling as though it were a floor. Properties are not occupied 100 percent of the time. Tenants turn over, and units sit vacant during re-leasing. Owners pay property taxes, insurance, maintenance, property management fees, capital expenditure reserves, and sometimes HOA dues. What remains after all of those costs is a materially different number than what the rent roll shows.

Operating Expenses and Why Gross Rent Is Not Income

Operating expenses are the costs of owning and operating the property, excluding debt service. They typically include property taxes, insurance, property management fees, maintenance and routine repairs, capital expenditure reserves (the budget for roofs, HVAC, appliances, and other systems that wear out over time), vacancy loss, and HOA dues where applicable.

The sum of those costs can vary significantly depending on the property's age, condition, location, management structure, and local tax environment, but in most residential investment scenarios they represent a meaningful portion of gross rent. Gross rent minus operating expenses produces a figure called **net operating income (NOI)**. NOI is the income a property generates from operations before debt service is factored in, and it is the number used in cap rate calculations.

The common version of this mistake is the buyer who calculates $2,200 per month in rent on a $340,000 property and immediately concludes the investment works because the rent covers the mortgage. What did not enter that calculation is property taxes, insurance, the property manager's fee, the six-week vacancy between tenants, the water heater that failed in year two, and the roof that is approaching the end of its useful life. Those costs are not hypothetical. They are the operating reality of owning an income property, and they are absent from any analysis built on gross rent alone.

Cap Rate

Capitalization rate (cap rate) is net operating income divided by purchase price or property value.

Cap rate = NOI / Purchase Price

A 4.8 percent cap rate expresses the property's operating income as a percentage of its price, before accounting for how the purchase is financed. The figure is useful for comparing similar properties within the same market at the same point in time, and for tracking how a market is pricing income relative to property value over a period of years. If cap rates in a specific segment have compressed from 5.5 percent to 4.1 percent over five years, the market has been paying progressively more per dollar of NOI, which means buyers have been accepting lower current income relative to price.

What cap rate cannot tell you, on its own, is whether the investment is rational. That requires understanding the assumptions behind the number, the financing structure the buyer will use, the investor's required return, and what the market expects in terms of future rent growth and appreciation. The most persistent misreading of cap rate is treating it as a verdict: high is good, low is bad. That reading misses what cap rates actually reflect.

High Cap Rate and Low Cap Rate Markets

Cap rates are partly an income measure and partly a market-expectation signal. The level of a cap rate in a given market or asset class reflects what investors are collectively pricing for income, risk, growth potential, liquidity, asset quality, and long-term exit value. Two markets with different cap rates are not simply offering better or worse deals; they are reflecting different combinations of those factors.

A low cap rate market can indicate that investors are accepting lower current income because they expect something else in return: stronger long-term appreciation, higher rent growth, greater liquidity, lower perceived risk, scarcity of quality inventory, or more predictable demand from a deep tenant pool. An investor who buys at a 4 percent cap rate in a supply-constrained market with strong employment and demographic tailwinds may be making a rational decision even if the current income looks thin, because a significant portion of the expected return may arrive through appreciation and rent growth over the holding period.

A high cap rate market can indicate that investors are being compensated today because they are accepting more uncertainty about tomorrow: weaker appreciation expectations, higher perceived risk, lower liquidity, slower employment or population growth, or greater management demands. An investor who buys at a 7 or 8 percent cap rate in a secondary market may be making a rational decision if the current income yield is sufficient to compensate for the risk profile and the investor does not need meaningful appreciation to meet their return threshold.

Neither cap rate level is automatically the better position. What changes is the return profile: how much of the expected total return comes from current income versus future appreciation, and whether that balance fits the investor's strategy, timeline, liquidity needs, and risk tolerance.

Cash Flow and Why Financing Matters

Where cap rate ignores financing, **cash flow** accounts for it. Cash flow is what remains after operating expenses and annual debt service have both been paid.

Cash flow = NOI minus annual debt service

Two investors can purchase the same property at the same price, with the same NOI, and produce completely different cash flow outcomes based on how they financed the acquisition. The investor with a lower rate, a larger down payment, or a shorter amortization period pays less in debt service and retains more cash flow. The investor with a higher rate or more leverage pays more in debt service and retains less, or may generate negative cash flow even when the property's operating performance looks acceptable.

This is why no cash flow analysis is complete without specific financing assumptions stated explicitly. Gross rent does not tell you cash flow. NOI does not tell you cash flow. Only NOI minus the actual debt service at the actual loan amount, rate, and term produces a reliable cash flow figure for a specific investor and a specific transaction.

Cash-on-Cash Return and Leverage

Cash-on-cash return measures annual pre-tax cash flow relative to the total cash the investor put into the purchase.

Cash-on-cash return = Annual cash flow / Total cash invested

Two investors who buy the same property at the same price and generate the same NOI will report different cash-on-cash returns if they used different amounts of equity. The investor who put in more cash earns a lower cash-on-cash return than the investor who used more debt, assuming both produce positive cash flow, because more of the return is distributed across more invested dollars.

Leverage amplifies both outcomes. An investor who uses debt to finance most of the purchase magnifies cash-on-cash return when the property performs above the cost of debt, and magnifies the loss when it performs below. This is not an argument for or against leverage; it is an argument for understanding exactly which direction leverage is pushing the analysis in any specific case.

Appreciation-Driven Versus Income-Driven Investing

Some investors buy income; others buy appreciation; most accept a blend of the two and understand that the balance between them shapes the total return and the risk profile.

An investor buying primarily for appreciation may accept thin or even negative current cash flow because they expect the property's value to increase, rents to grow, or both. That strategy concentrates risk on the future. If appreciation does not materialize, if the exit environment is unfavorable when the investor needs to sell, or if rates rise substantially and refinancing becomes costly, the thin cash flow provides no cushion and may require the investor to fund the property from other sources during the holding period.

An investor buying primarily for income wants current yield and places less weight on what the property will be worth in a decade. That strategy reduces dependence on favorable exit conditions but may leave performance on the table in markets where long-term appreciation has historically outpaced income yield.

Neither strategy is universally correct. What determines which is appropriate for a specific investor is their timeline, liquidity requirements, tax situation, leverage tolerance, and risk capacity, none of which are visible in a cap rate or a gross rent figure.

How Assumptions Change the Conclusion

Investment analysis is highly sensitive to its inputs. A property that appears to produce modest positive cash flow under one set of assumptions may bleed cash under a different set. This is not a flaw in the framework; it is a feature that requires precision and penalizes optimistic or imprecise underwriting.

Example: An investor is analyzing a single-family rental listed at \$487,000. The property rents for \$2,750 per month under the current lease, or \$33,000 per year at full occupancy. The investor estimates annual operating expenses at \$11,400: property taxes, insurance, a property management fee at 9 percent of collected rent (about $2,970 at this rent), a maintenance reserve, and a capital expenditure reserve for aging systems. Rent minus those expenses leaves net operating income of $21,600. At the asking price, that is a cap rate of approximately 4.44 percent ($21,600 ÷ $487,000).

The investor puts 25 percent down, or $121,750, and finances the remaining $365,250 at a 7.0 percent rate on a 30-year fixed loan. That loan carries annual debt service of approximately $29,160. With NOI of $21,600 against debt service of $29,160, cash flow is approximately negative $7,560 per year before taxes. The property earns less from operations than it costs to carry, because a 4.44 percent operating yield cannot cover 7.0 percent debt.

A second investor, evaluating the same property on the same day, reaches a different conclusion because he changes two inputs. He expects rent to rise to $3,100 per month, or $37,200 per year, when the lease renews in five months. That higher rent also lifts the one expense tied to it: the 9 percent management fee climbs from about $2,970 to about $3,348, bringing operating expenses to roughly $11,778. His projected NOI is therefore about $25,422, and at the asking price that is a forward cap rate of approximately 5.22 percent ($25,422 ÷ $487,000).

He also plans to put 30 percent down, which reduces the loan to $340,900 and annual debt service to approximately $27,216. Against projected NOI of $25,422, his forward cash flow is approximately negative $1,794 per year, a materially better position than the first investor's, though still negative. He is willing to cover the small shortfall because his expected rent trajectory, combined with expected appreciation over a five- to seven-year hold, meets his required return.

Same property, same asking price, same day, two defensible analyses and two different conclusions about whether the deal works. Neither investor is wrong within their own framework. What differs is their assumptions about rent, their financing structure, and their return requirements, and each of those assumptions moves the result.

The practical implication for agents is that investor buyers are not all running the same math. Understanding which assumptions are driving the analysis, and whether those assumptions are grounded in what the local rental market actually supports, is how an agent provides useful input rather than simply facilitating a transaction built on optimistic projections.

How Investor Demand Affects Residential Market Segments

Investor activity is not evenly distributed across the residential market. It concentrates in specific segments: entry-level single-family homes with strong tenant demand, small multifamily properties up to four units, properties near employment centers or universities, and homes with short-term rental potential where local regulation permits it.

When investor demand concentrates in a segment, it can compete directly with owner-occupant buyers for the same inventory. In those moments, the first-time buyer may be competing with a buyer whose valuation logic, financing, and speed of decision are structured around income yield rather than personal use.

The relationship runs the other direction as well. When financing costs rise sharply or when cap rates in a market no longer support investor return requirements, investor demand can exit a segment relatively quickly. When it does, segments that were partially sustained by investor activity may see softer absorption and wider inventory, which affects pricing for all buyers in that segment including owner-occupants.

What Agents Should and Should Not Do With Investment Metrics

Understanding these metrics does not make an agent an investment analyst. It makes an agent a more effective communicator with investor clients, a more informed listing agent when a property will attract investor interest, and a more accurate interpreter of market behavior in segments where investor demand is a meaningful variable.

Agents should be able to explain the difference between gross rent and NOI, recognize when a client's investment thesis rests on assumptions that may not hold in the local market, and communicate why cap rate is not a simple score. They should not provide tax advice, legal advice, securities advice, or detailed investment underwriting beyond their competence, license, and brokerage policy. Exact boundaries vary by state and situation. When a conversation moves into depreciation analysis, 1031 exchange strategy, complex leveraged structures, or individualized investment advice, the appropriate referral is to a qualified advisor, attorney, or CPA.

The clearest professional exposure in investment-adjacent conversations is not making an analytical mistake; it is overstepping the scope of what a real estate license authorizes. Understanding these metrics clarifies where the boundary is, not just how to approach it.

The useful professional position is narrow but valuable: know the language well enough to ask better questions, catch unsupported assumptions, and keep the conversation in the right lane. If the rent assumption looks too high for the local market, say that. If the expense estimate ignores management, vacancy, or reserves, point out the missing category. If the client wants advice about tax treatment, securities rules, or whether the investment is appropriate for their broader financial life, bring in the right specialist.

Market Literacy Takeaway

An investor is not buying a home. An investor is buying a set of assumptions about rent, expenses, financing, appreciation, and exit value, packaged into a current price. The same property can be a rational buy under one set of assumptions and an obvious pass under another.

Use This When

- An investor buyer asks why the cap rate on a listing looks low compared to their expectations or their previous market
- A listing will attract both owner-occupant and investor interest and you need to understand both pricing logics to advise the seller accurately
- A client cites gross rent as the primary argument for why a property is priced correctly or is a good deal
- A market update needs to explain why investor demand has increased, decreased, or shifted within a specific price segment
- A seller with a tenanted property needs to understand how investor buyers will evaluate the asset differently than owner-occupants who are comparing it to vacant homes nearby
- An investor client's underwriting assumptions seem disconnected from what the local rental market actually supports

Be Careful When

- Treating cap rate as a simple "higher is better" or "lower is worse" metric without accounting for market type, perceived risk, growth expectations, liquidity, and asset quality

• Confusing gross rent with NOI or cash flow; operating expenses can absorb a meaningful share of gross rent before debt service is even considered

• Presenting a cash flow estimate without stating the specific financing assumptions behind it; two buyers with different loan terms will see different cash flow on the same property

• Providing tax, legal, or investment advisory guidance beyond your licensure; investment analysis informs the conversation, it does not replace the need for qualified advisors

• Comparing cap rates across fundamentally different markets, property types, or risk profiles without acknowledging that the cap rate difference may reflect growth and risk differences rather than mispricing

• Treating investment analysis as a closed calculation; every output is only as reliable as the assumptions driving it, and small changes in rent, vacancy, or rate can change the conclusion materially

Client Explanation

When an investor evaluates a rental property, the math starts with gross rent but does not stop there. Operating expenses, vacancy, and the cost of the loan all come out before anything resembling cash flow is on the table. The cap rate tells you the operating income relative to price, before financing, and it is useful for comparing similar properties in the same market, but it does not tell you whether the deal works for a specific buyer because that depends entirely on their loan terms, down payment, and what return they require. Two investors can buy the same property at the same price and have completely different outcomes based on how they financed it and what they were expecting the property to do.

CHAPTER 18

How to Build a Market Read

A market dashboard can be full and still say almost nothing useful on its own. Median price is up year over year. Inventory is higher than it was last spring. Days on market is creeping up. Mortgage rates are elevated. Price reductions are more common in the mid-market. Well-positioned homes are still moving. Every one of those signals may be accurate, current, and worth knowing. A list of them is still not a market read.

The problem is not usually that the professional has too little information. It is that the information has not yet been sorted into a decision. A market read begins when someone decides which of those signals belongs to the decision in front of them, which ones are background context, which ones are in tension with each other, and what practical recommendation follows from the combination. Until that happens, the dashboard is only a collection of numbers that describe the market from different angles without yet telling a seller how to price, a buyer how to negotiate, or a brokerage where conditions are actually changing.

This is where a lot of market analysis quietly fails. The professional may have all the relevant tabs open, all the familiar metrics pulled, and all the current reports sitting in front of them, but the work is not finished when the data is assembled. The work begins when the question is identified, the relevant signals are selected, and the conflicting ones are resolved into advice specific enough to act on. A market read is not a data dump. It is the act of turning separate signals into judgment for a specific decision.

Start With the Decision, Not the Dashboard

The most reliable way to build a useful market read is to start with the question before opening the data. Different decisions require different evidence, and the most common mistake in market analysis is pulling everything available and then searching for a conclusion rather than identifying the question first and then selecting the signals that answer it.

A seller pricing question is not asking for a market summary. It is asking how buyers are likely to respond to this property, in this segment, at this price, if it enters the market now. A buyer negotiation question is not asking whether the market is generally strong or weak. It is asking where leverage actually sits on this property relative to its competing alternatives. An investor analysis question is asking something different again. A brokerage strategy question is different from all of them.

None of those questions is answered by the same set of indicators. Collecting everything before knowing the question produces a report. Starting with the decision and then pulling the evidence that belongs to it is what produces a market read.

Select the Relevant Lenses

Earlier, Chapter 02 separated the market into six lenses: price, supply, demand, velocity, affordability, and listing performance. You do not need to rebuild that full framework every time you prepare for a conversation. You need to decide which of those lenses belongs to the decision in front of you, which ones are useful background context, and which ones are not carrying much weight in this situation.

A seller pricing decision usually pulls hardest from supply, velocity, listing performance, and affordability. You need to know how many competing listings are active, how quickly well-priced homes are moving, how frequently sellers in the segment are reducing, and whether current financing conditions have narrowed the buyer pool enough to make pricing errors more expensive than they would have been a year earlier.

A buyer negotiation decision usually pulls from velocity, supply, and listing performance. The relevant question is not whether inventory is up in the abstract. It is whether similar homes are still clearing quickly, whether this listing has already missed its strongest market window, and whether the seller has been getting the kind of response that creates negotiating room or the kind that still supports firm pricing.

Sometimes the decision requires a more specialized input. If builder inventory is competing directly with resale, the new-construction signals in Chapter 16 belong in the read. If the decision is investor-driven, the income and return measures in Chapter 17 belong in the read. Those are not replacement categories. They are specialized tools pulled in when the decision actually requires them.

Start With the Decision Question

Decision Question	Key Signal Categories	Watch Most Closely	Practical Output
Seller Pricing	Supply, velocity, listing performance	Current competition, DOM, price reductions	List price and reduction plan
Buyer Leverage	Supply, velocity, listing performance	Stale listings vs. fresh demand, price ratios	Offer posture
Investor Analysis	Rent, expenses, cap rate	NOI, debt service, risk	Financial return analysis
Brokerage Strategy	Inventory, velocity, rates	Where pressure is building	Marketing and business strategy
Market Update	Price, supply, demand	Broader trends vs. segment trends	Client-ready explanations

The most useful market reads are the ones that make the clearest selections. A seller pricing analysis that includes cap rates and investor absorption metrics has included signals that do not belong to the decision, which adds noise rather than clarity. A buyer negotiation analysis that leads with the year-over-year median without addressing pending activity and days-on-market distribution in the buyer's specific price band still has not answered the question the buyer is actually asking.

Resolve Contradictory Signals

Chapter 02 already established that different lenses can point in different directions at the same time. Building a market read means deciding how those readings relate rather than treating contradiction as a problem that needs to be hidden.

Markets routinely show rising prices alongside rising inventory, increasing days on market alongside still-strong absorption in certain segments, and constrained affordability alongside resilient demand from buyers who have adjusted their price range rather than exited the market. None of these combinations is self-contradictory if the underlying dynamics are understood.

A market where median price is up year over year, inventory is building, days on market is rising in the mid-price tier, and affordability is constrained by elevated rates is not simply a good market or a bad market. It is a market where well-priced inventory in strong-demand price bands is still clearing, where the mid-market seller who prices aspirationally rather than accurately is increasingly exposed to extended market time and eventual reduction, and where buyers have more options than a year ago but less purchasing power, which means selection is more careful rather than less urgent. That is a market read. It accounts for the apparent contradiction rather than resolving it by choosing the signal that supports the preferred conclusion.

The professional failure is not encountering contradictory signals. It is reporting each one separately without explaining how they relate, or selecting the signals that validate a predetermined recommendation and ignoring the ones that complicate it.

Apply the Segment Filter

Every market read should be segmented to the level of specificity the decision requires. Chapter 02 made the conceptual point. Here the operational point is simpler: if the decision is specific, the data has to become specific too. Metro-area or county data is context. Segment data is where the advice starts.

A metro-area median that is up does not mean that every price band is up. A metro-area inventory figure that is rising does not mean that every product type is accumulating supply at the same rate. A metro-area days-on-market figure that is increasing does not mean that every neighborhood is softening equally.

The relevant segmentation filters are geography, price band, property type, condition, and buyer pool. A condominium in a transit-adjacent urban neighborhood competes in a different sub-market than a single-family home in a suburban school district at the same price point. A property in above-average condition in a price band where most inventory is dated competes for a different buyer than an as-is listing in the same band. Each of those distinctions changes which lenses belong in the read and what the resulting signals mean.

A listing appointment for a mid-market single-family home in a specific school district requires a market read filtered to that product type, in that geography, at that price band. The metro-area headline is background. The segment data is the read.

Separate Signal From Noise

Not every movement in market data reflects a durable change in market conditions. Some variation is seasonal, some is statistical, and some is the result of a single week's data carrying more weight than a single week should.

A one-month rise in days on market during a period that is seasonally slower is not evidence of softening. It may simply be evidence of what happens every year in that market during that period. A one-month jump in new listings during early spring is not a supply surge; it is spring. A single sale at a price significantly above or below the cluster of recent comparable sales is not a new market signal; it is an outlier that will distort any ratio that includes it without adjustment.

Separating signal from noise requires a longer window, a comparison to the same period in prior years, and an understanding of what normal seasonal patterns look like in the relevant sub-market. A rising days-on-market trend across six consecutive months is a signal. A rising days-on-market figure in October compared to July is almost always noise. A market read that cannot make that distinction is only naming movement, not interpreting it.

A Market Read for a Seller Pricing Decision

Example: An agent is preparing to list a three-bedroom single-family home in a mid-market price band. She pulls the signals most relevant to the seller's pricing decision.

Median price in the metro area is up approximately 5 percent year over year. Active inventory in the metro area has increased relative to last spring. In the seller's specific price band and school district, however, the picture is more precise: days on market for closed sales has increased from an average of 11 days six months ago to an average of 22 days over the most recent 60-day period. Price reductions are appearing in roughly 30 percent of active listings at this price band, up from approximately 12 percent in the same window last year. The close-to-original-list ratio in this segment has compressed from 99.1 percent to 96.3 percent over the same period. Well-presented homes with accurate launch pricing are still going under contract, but within 18 to 28 days rather than the 7 to 12 days common in the prior year. Overpriced listings are sitting past the first market window, accumulating days on market, and eventually reducing.

The mortgage rate environment has reduced the size of the qualified buyer pool relative to 18 months ago. Buyers who remain in the market are more deliberate about value because they are financing at a higher rate and have less appetite for paying a premium and then negotiating repairs.

The market read for this seller is not "the market is good" or "the market is bad." The market read is: buyers are still active in this segment, but they are less forgiving of pricing errors than they were a year ago. A listing that enters at an aspirational price is unlikely to generate the competitive offer environment that would have been possible 18 months ago. The first two weeks on market are the highest-leverage window, and recovering from a stale start at this stage of the cycle requires a reduction that typically lands below where an accurate initial price would have been. The recommendation that follows from that read is to price accurately at launch, present the property well, and respond quickly to early feedback rather than waiting for buyer urgency to correct an overpriced position.

A Market Read for a Buyer Timing Decision

Example: A buyer is tracking active listings in her target price band and has watched inventory rise over the past three months. She interprets rising inventory as evidence that she has negotiating leverage on any listing she chooses.

The agent pulls a more segmented read. Active inventory has risen overall, but pending sales in the buyer's price band are also up relative to the prior period, indicating that absorption is keeping pace with the supply increase. The pending-to-active ratio in her specific segment is 0.41: for every 100 active listings, 41 are matched by contracts in process, a figure that suggests buyers are still choosing actively rather than deferring in large numbers. Well-priced listings in this band have been going under contract within 14 days on average. The inventory that has built is concentrated in two sub-groups: listings that entered overpriced and have been sitting without reduction, and listings in condition categories where buyers are applying higher scrutiny given current financing costs.

The market read for this buyer is not "inventory is up, so you have leverage." The market read is: leverage exists, but it is concentrated in specific situations. On accurately priced, well-presented listings, the competition is still present and days on market is short. On stale listings and overpriced listings, there is room to negotiate. Treating all available inventory as equally negotiable is likely to produce offers that lose on well-positioned homes and succeed only on the homes with the clearest problems.

Turn the Read Into Advice

A market read that cannot be translated into a specific recommendation has not yet done its job. The output is not "the market is complex" or "conditions are mixed." Those are observations about the data. The output is a specific, decision-oriented statement: a price range, a timing assessment, a negotiation posture, a positioning strategy, or a risk acknowledgment.

For a seller, the translation might be: "Given what the segment is showing us, I recommend a list price of $X, which positions us ahead of the most recent reductions and within the range where absorption is still strong. If we are not under contract within the first three weeks, the data suggests we revisit pricing rather than waiting for a delayed buyer." That is actionable. It tells the seller what to do, on what timeline, with what contingency.

For a buyer, the translation might be: "The listing at $X has been on the market for 41 days with no reduction, which puts it in the category where the seller is more likely to negotiate. I would recommend an offer in the range of $Y with this justification." That is actionable for a different reason: it is specific to the property and the market position, not a general observation about inventory.

The market read is the analysis. The advice is the translation. Both are required for the agent to have done the job.

If the output cannot be stated as a next step, the read is not finished. "Conditions are mixed" may be true, but it does not help the client act. "Conditions are mixed, and because buyer selectivity is showing up most clearly in overpriced listings, we should launch inside the segment-supported range and revisit quickly if early traffic is thin" is a market read turned into advice.

Market Literacy Takeaway

A market read begins with a decision, not a dashboard. The job is to choose the signals that belong to that decision, explain what they mean together, and turn the result into advice specific enough to act on.

Use This When

- Preparing for any seller listing appointment where a pricing recommendation needs to be grounded in segment-level evidence rather than metro-area headlines
- A buyer asks whether now is a good time to act or wait, and the answer requires distinguishing between overall market direction and segment-specific conditions
- Presenting a market update to a brokerage, team, or client audience and determining which signals to lead with
- A set of indicators appears to point in different directions and needs to be reconciled into a coherent interpretation before advising a client
- A client is making a pricing or timing decision based on one statistic seen online or in a news report
- Evaluating a segment where conditions at the sub-market level differ from conditions at the metro-area level

Be Careful When

- Reporting multiple statistics sequentially and calling that a market read; data without interpretation is information, not advice
- Using metro-area or county-level statistics to advise on a decision that is segment-specific by price band, property type, and geography
- Resolving a contradiction between indicators by selecting the one that supports a predetermined conclusion; contradiction is information about the market, not an inconvenience to be set aside
- Treating a seasonal pattern as structural change or interpreting a single month's movement as evidence of a new trend
- Presenting a market read with more certainty than the available signals can actually support; acknowledge when the signals are genuinely mixed or when a longer observation window is needed before the direction is clear
- Letting a client's preferred conclusion drive indicator selection; choosing signals because they support what the client wants to hear rather than because they are most relevant to the question

Client Explanation

The statistics I showed you each tell a partial story, and some of them seem to point in different directions. What I have done is look at the signals that are most relevant to your specific situation, in your price range, in your neighborhood, and figure out what they mean together. That combination is the market read, and it is more useful than any single number because it is filtered for your decision rather than built to describe the whole market at once. The recommendation that follows from it is the specific thing you can actually act on.

CHAPTER 19

How to Explain the Market to Clients

Most clients are not walking into market conversations with no information. They are walking in with disconnected information, pieces gathered from headlines, portal statistics, lender comments, neighbor stories, social media clips, coworker anecdotes, and partial market reports that were never built to answer the same question. What they often bring with them is a conclusion that feels informed because it has several inputs behind it, even if none of those inputs was selected for the decision the client is actually trying to make.

That is why these conversations go sideways so easily. The individual pieces are often accurate. The problem is not that the client knows nothing. The problem is that the pieces are arriving without hierarchy, without segmentation, and without any framework that distinguishes broad market context from decision-specific evidence. A metro-area inventory headline gets treated as if it answers a neighborhood pricing question. A coworker's below-asking purchase gets treated as if it answers whether this buyer has leverage on this house. A national economist's outlook gets treated as if it answers what should happen in a specific price band over the next 30 days.

Explaining the market to clients is not data recitation. It is translation. The job is to take the signal that actually belongs to the decision, connect it to the recommendation that follows, and remove the noise that makes the client feel informed without actually becoming oriented. Until that translation happens, more information usually makes the conversation harder, not easier.

Why Clients Have Information Without Interpretation

Real estate information has become widely available in a way that has not made it easier to use. Clients can find median price, inventory count, days on market, and price-change trends before they speak to an agent. They encounter market commentary from economists, journalists, and social media sources whose analyses may be accurate about one thing and inapplicable to another. They hear from friends, family members, and colleagues whose transactions happened in different price bands, different product types, or different geographic sub-markets than the one they are actually navigating.

The result is a common client profile: someone who has assembled a collection of valid data points that do not connect into a coherent picture of their specific situation. The individual facts are defensible. The composite conclusion drawn from them is often wrong for the decision at hand.

An agent who responds to this by dismissing the client's research loses credibility. An agent who validates it without correcting the misapplication allows the client to proceed from a flawed premise. The third option is translation: accepting the facts the client has found, explaining what they actually measure, and redirecting to the evidence that is most relevant to the decision.

The Agent's Role Is Translation

The agent's role in a market explanation is not to present data, and it is not to simplify data until it is comfortable. The role is to translate: to take a market read built from the right signals for the question, and render it in language that connects the evidence to the decision.

Translation is not the same as dumbing down. A simplified explanation that omits the relevant nuance has failed the client even if it is easy to understand. An explanation that accurately describes a complex market condition in plain language, at the level of detail required to guide the specific decision, has done the job.

The practical test is whether the explanation changes what the client does next. An explanation that leaves the client with an accurate impression of market conditions but no clearer sense of what to do is a description, not a translation. A translation ends with a recommendation the client can act on and a reason for it the client can explain to someone else.

Simplifying Without Distorting

There is a meaningful difference between an explanation that is simple and one that is misleading. The simplification failure mode that damages client trust most is not complexity: it is false certainty. An agent who says "the market is great, prices only go up" is not simplifying; they are distorting. An agent who says "this is a buyer's market" about a market where leverage exists only in specific segments is not simplifying; they are mischaracterizing.

Plain language is not the problem. Imprecision is.

The discipline of simplifying without distorting requires the agent to identify what must be accurate in the explanation and what can safely be left out. For a seller, the precise calculation behind months' supply can usually be left out; what must be accurate is the direction and the implication for pricing strategy. For a buyer, the technical definition of a close-to-list ratio can usually be left out; what must be accurate is what that ratio is saying about whether competition is present in this price band. The metric's name and formula are often optional. The metric's directional implication for the decision is not.

Start With the Decision

Every effective market explanation begins with the question the client is actually trying to answer, not with the data the agent has assembled. The data exists to serve the question. If the question is not established first, the explanation starts in the wrong place.

A seller preparing to list needs to know how the current market will respond to their specific pricing strategy. An explanation that begins with metro-area median price and works forward to their home requires the client to make the translation at every step. An explanation that begins with what buyers in their segment are currently paying for homes like theirs, and then supplies the market context that explains why, requires no translation. The client hears their question answered, supported by evidence, in that order.

A buyer weighing an offer needs to know whether they have leverage on this home, at this price, given current competition. An explanation that begins with a metro-area inventory figure and expects the client to derive their negotiating posture from it has reversed the order. An explanation that begins with the absorption rate and days on market for this property type, in this geography, at this price band, and then situates that within the broader market context, reaches the client's question first.

Start with the decision. Supply the context that explains and supports the recommendation. Let the market data appear in service of the answer, not ahead of it.

Market Context and Property-Specific Advice Are Not the Same Thing

One of the most persistent client communication errors is conflating market context with property-level advice. They are different things, they answer different questions, and delivering them in the wrong order creates confusion rather than clarity.

Market context describes the broad conditions: what is happening to inventory, prices, rates, and buyer activity across the relevant market area. It answers the question "what kind of market is this?" Property-specific advice describes the strategy for a specific listing or offer based on the segment-level evidence for that home. It answers the question "what should we do here?"

A seller whose home is in a segment where absorption is still strong does not need to hear that the broader metro area is softening before hearing the pricing recommendation. A seller whose home is in a segment where days on market is rising and reductions are more common needs that market context before the recommendation, because the recommendation will require explanation. The sequence is not arbitrary; it follows from what the client needs to understand in order for the recommendation to make sense.

Handling Uncertainty Without Sounding Weak

Markets contain genuine uncertainty, and clients deserve to know when an agent's recommendation depends on assumptions that may not hold. Projecting false certainty does more damage to the relationship in the long run than acknowledging the limits of the available evidence.

The skill is not avoiding uncertainty. The skill is calibrating it. "I don't know what rates will do" tells the client nothing useful and invites doubt about whether the agent knows anything. "Rates have been moving with bond-market expectations rather than Fed announcements, which means the direction over the next 60 days is genuinely unclear. What we do know is what your payment looks like at current rates, and we can build the strategy around the rate you can actually lock today rather than one you might get later" is honest about what is unknown and immediately redirects to what can be acted on.

The structure of calibrated uncertainty is: here is what we do not know, here is what the data does show, and here is how the strategy accounts for both. Clients who hear that structure do not conclude the agent is unsure. They conclude the agent has thought carefully about the risk.

Explaining Contradictory Signals

Clients who encounter contradictory market signals often conclude that the market is simply confusing, or that whoever assembled the data made an error, or that the picture is too uncertain to act on. The agent who can explain why the contradiction exists, rather than argue that it does not, provides a service that most clients have not received before.

A market with rising prices and longer days on market is not contradictory; it is a market where sellers are pricing into appreciation and buyers are pushing back, meaning the most recent comps are closing but taking longer and sitting at a lower percentage of original list price than they did a year ago. A market with rising inventory and still-strong absorption is not contradictory; it is a market where supply and demand are both expanding, and velocity is holding even as the count grows. The explanation behind the apparent contradiction is usually the most useful piece of market literacy an agent can deliver.

The one error to avoid is using the contradiction to support whatever conclusion is most convenient. If inventory is up and prices are up, the explanation is not "well, both are true, so you can take your pick." The explanation is the mechanism that connects them: what kind of inventory is rising, where demand is concentrated, and what the combination implies for this buyer or seller.

Tailoring the Explanation by Client Type

Sellers, buyers, investors, and broader audiences are asking different questions, and the same market condition requires a different framing for each.

A seller needs to understand what current conditions mean for the price they should set and the timeline they should expect. The explanation should be grounded in what buyers in their segment are actually paying, what is competing with their home, and how long well-positioned inventory is taking to close. Broad market context supports the recommendation but should not dominate it.

A buyer needs to understand where their leverage is strong and where it is not, and what the current supply and velocity mean for how quickly they need to decide. The explanation should distinguish between the market overall and the specific segment they are shopping in, and should be honest about where competition is still present.

An investor needs the income and return question answered: whether the price, rent, expense, and financing assumptions still produce a viable return profile, and what the cap rate environment is saying about how other investors are pricing risk and growth in this market. The explanation connects market mechanics to investment math, which is a different translation from anything a traditional buyer or seller needs.

A broader audience, a team meeting, a brokerage briefing, or a client group event requires the clearest explanation: the one that requires no specialized vocabulary, focuses on the one or two signals most relevant to the questions the audience has, and ends with a clear direction rather than a survey of everything happening in the market.

Three Hypothetical Explanations

For a seller whose home is in a rising market that is also becoming more selective:

Example: A seller says that prices are up year over year in the metro area and her home should be priced above the most recent comps.

A better explanation: "The market being up overall is useful context for where values are heading. But the pricing strategy for your home has to come from what buyers are choosing between right now, in your price band and your neighborhood, not from the metro-area trend. When we look at the segment your home competes in, days on market has increased over the past 60 days, and price reductions are more common than they were a year ago. Well-presented homes are still moving, but buyers are less forgiving of pricing errors than they were in the prior cycle. That means an accurate launch price is more valuable now than it would have been 18 months ago. Pricing above the comps increases the risk of a stale start, which typically results in a reduction that lands you below where an accurate initial price would have been."

That explanation uses the metro-area trend as context, then grounds the recommendation in segment-level evidence. The client hears both, in the right order, and understands why the recommendation is not simply applying the headline trend to her home.

For a buyer who believes rising inventory means universal leverage:

Example: A buyer sees that active inventory in the metro area has increased and concludes she has negotiating leverage on every home she considers.

A better explanation: "Inventory is higher than it was, and that does give buyers more options than they had at the peak. But leverage is not evenly distributed across everything available. When we look at your price band specifically, absorption is still strong, and well-priced move-in-ready listings are moving within two to three weeks. The leverage you are looking for exists mainly on two categories: listings that have been sitting past their first market window, and listings that came in overpriced and have not reduced yet. On those, there is room to negotiate. On a well-positioned new listing, the competition is still present and the offer strategy needs to reflect that."

That explanation validates what the client found, redirects to the segment-level data, and gives her a usable framework for calibrating her strategy property by property rather than applying a single posture to everything she considers.

For an investor reading contradictory signals:

Example: An investor sees that cap rates, rent growth rates, and mortgage rates are each moving in different directions and asks whether this is a good or bad market to buy in.

A better explanation: "The question is not whether the market is good or bad overall. The question is whether this specific property, at this specific price, with your financing structure and hold period, produces a return that meets your threshold. Cap rates in this market are reflecting both the rate environment and investor expectations about long-term appreciation and rent growth. If those expectations hold, the math works at this cap rate. If rent growth is slower than expected or exit cap rates widen, it does not. The job right now is to stress-test the assumptions that are doing the most work in your underwriting, not to wait for the signals to stop moving in different directions."

That explanation does not pretend the signals are simple or aligned. It redirects the investor to the actual analytical question and gives a clear direction for what to examine next.

Repeatable Language Without Sounding Scripted

The strongest market explanations are ones the client can repeat accurately to a spouse, partner, attorney, or another decision-maker later that day. An explanation that requires the agent to be in the room to make sense is not yet finished. An explanation that can travel does its job beyond the meeting.

This does not mean agents should develop a script and recite it to every client in the same words. It means the conceptual structure of the explanation should be consistent: market context first, segment-level evidence second, specific recommendation third. The language can and should adapt to the client, but the logical sequence should not.

An agent who tells one seller "it's a seller's market" and tells another seller the same market is "balanced" has not achieved consistency. An agent who tells every seller "the broad market tells us where values are heading; the segment-level data tells us what your home is competing against right now; the strategy follows from the second, not the first" has a repeatable framework that clients can use to understand each explanation they receive.

The practical test is simple: after the meeting, could the client repeat the logic without you standing next to them? If the answer is yes, the explanation was probably clear enough. If the answer is no, the client may have heard the conclusion without understanding the reasoning that supports it.

Market Literacy Takeaway

The best market explanation is not the most complete one. It is the one that makes the next decision clearer. Clients need the part of the market that changes what they should do, delivered at the level of precision that guides action, not the full dataset that produces confusion.

Use This When

- A client arrives with assembled market information drawn from news, social media, friends, or online data that does not connect to their actual situation
- A seller believes the metro-area trend applies directly to their home's pricing strategy
- A buyer believes rising inventory means equal leverage on every available listing
- A market explanation needs to acknowledge genuine uncertainty

while still producing a usable recommendation

- Preparing for any client meeting where market conditions will inform a pricing, offer, or timing decision
- A client asks for a market update and you need to give them something more actionable than a summary of current statistics

Be Careful When

- Presenting every available metric in sequence and treating that as a market explanation; data without direction is a report, not a recommendation
- Oversimplifying to the point that the explanation stops being accurate; plain language and precision are not opposites
- Projecting false certainty about pricing outcomes, rate direction, timing, or negotiation results; acknowledge what is genuinely unknown and explain how the strategy accounts for it
- Treating market context as property advice; the metro-area trend does not price the house, and the broad conditions do not determine the offer strategy for a specific listing
- Validating a client's assembled data without correcting the misapplication; agree that the facts are true, then redirect to what they mean for this specific decision in this specific segment
- Using the same phrasing with every client to the point that it sounds rehearsed; keep the logical sequence consistent but let the language adapt to the conversation

Client Explanation

What you have found is accurate, and I want to use it. The way it connects to your specific decision is the part I want to walk through with you, because each of those facts describes a different layer of the market, and some of them apply directly to your situation while others describe conditions in segments that do not affect your price range or your timeline. The broader metro-area picture gives us context. The segment-level data gives us the strategy. Let me show you what the evidence says in the part of the market where you are actually competing.

CHAPTER 20

The Market Literacy Advantage

By the end of most market conversations, the question is rarely whether the data exists. It usually does. The question is whether the person using it can separate the numbers that actually belong in the decision from the numbers that only make the conversation feel more informed.

Market data has become broadly accessible, and in many cases standardized enough that clients, agents, team leaders, brokers, and investors are often looking at some version of the same visible information. Median price, inventory trends, days on market, rate environments, price reductions, builder activity, and rent signals can all be pulled quickly by someone who knows where to look.

What remains uneven is judgment. The professional advantage lives in knowing which numbers belong in the decision, which ones are only background context, how the relevant signals interact, and what recommendation follows once those relationships are understood. Two professionals can begin with the same market summary and arrive at very different advice, not because one has secret data and the other does not, but because one has done the interpretive work and the other has only repeated the inputs.

Pricing and Positioning

The advantage shows up fastest in the listing appointment, because that is where a broad market story has to become a specific pricing recommendation.

An agent without a precise market read tends to treat a market trend as a pricing instruction. The metro-area median is up, so the listing should reflect that. Last year's close price, adjusted by the headline percentage, becomes the recommended list price. The advice sounds confident because it comes with a number. But the number is describing the aggregate, and the aggregate is almost always the wrong frame for a specific property, for reasons the earlier chapters in this book explain: composition shift, seasonality, segment divergence, sample size, and the distinction between what sold metro-wide and what is actually competing in the sub-market where this listing will live.

An agent with a precise read arrives at the conversation knowing what buyers in this price band, in this geography, for this product type have been paying, how quickly well-priced inventory has been moving, what the close-to-original-list ratio looks like in this segment, and how common price reductions have become in the past 60 days. The pricing recommendation comes from that analysis. The metro-area trend is context. The segment-level evidence is the answer.

The practical consequences are not subtle. A listing that enters the market accurately positioned will move through its first market window before buyer skepticism accumulates. A listing that enters overpriced will sit, acquire days on market visible to every future buyer as a signal of doubt, and eventually require a reduction that typically lands below where accurate initial pricing would have been. The professional use is straightforward: use broad market numbers to frame the conversation, then price from the segment that actually competes for the listing.

Negotiation and Timing

The same interpretive precision changes negotiation guidance, because buyers do not need a general market opinion nearly as much as they need to know where leverage is actually concentrated.

The agent who says "inventory is up, so you have leverage" has made a statement that is technically defensible and practically incomplete. Rising inventory does shift market conditions in a direction that often benefits buyers. But applying that condition uniformly to every available listing produces an offer strategy that is too blunt to be useful: it will lose competitive listings, succeed only on the ones with clear problems, and leave the buyer uncertain about why some offers worked and others did not.

The more precise version names what the data actually shows. Inventory is higher overall, but leverage depends on price band, condition, days on market, and whether similar homes in this segment are still absorbing quickly. On accurately priced, well-presented listings that entered the market recently, buyer competition remains. On listings that have sat past their first market window without a reduction, there is likely room to negotiate. On listings that entered overpriced and have not corrected, the seller has not yet accepted what the market is saying.

Timing questions expose the same difference. A buyer asking whether to wait for prices to drop does not need a headline answer. The useful read comes from distinguishing between seasonal softening and structural change, then connecting that distinction to the qualified buyer pool, the direction of days on market, and the way reductions are moving inside the relevant segment. The professional use is not to promise the next move perfectly. It is to tell the client where leverage exists now, what would need to change before the advice changes, and what kind of listing deserves a different posture.

Communication, Credibility, and Professional Judgment

Client communication is where the analysis either survives or collapses once the recommendation has to leave the room.

Clients notice the difference between an agent who summarized statistics and an agent who explained what those statistics mean for the decision in front of them. The summary produces a client who has heard some numbers. The explanation produces a client who understands the reasoning behind a specific recommendation and can relay that reasoning to a spouse, a co-decision maker, an attorney, or their own doubt at the end of a long day. The first client is relying on the agent's confidence. The second client has internalized the logic.

That is also where professional credibility becomes durable. An agent who can explain why a rising median does not mean every home appreciated, why rising inventory does not mean equal negotiating advantage on every listing, and why a price reduction at day 8 means something different from one at day 38 has conveyed a level of market understanding that no credential or title communicates independently. A client who questions the pricing recommendation receives an explanation that can withstand follow-up questions. A buyer's agent who disputes the negotiation posture receives a specific, grounded counterargument.

Even when the market moves against the recommendation, visible reasoning still helps. If the pricing recommendation misses because the composition of comparable sales shifted after the recommendation was made, the agent and client can identify that together and adjust. If the offer strategy failed because a competing buyer had information about the seller's timeline that was not available at the time, the next decision can be refined rather than guessed at again. The professional use is not certainty. It is having reasoning clear enough to defend, revise, and improve under pressure.

The applied advantage is not drama. It is the client leaving with a recommendation they understand well enough to use. In a listing appointment, that means the price is not just a number on a slide; it is the result of a visible read of the buyer pool, competing inventory, recent reductions, and market timing. In an offer conversation, the posture is not just "aggressive" or "strong"; it is tied to what this listing has shown the market so far.

Beyond the Transaction

That same interpretive discipline matters beyond a single file, because the professional question keeps repeating in slightly different forms: what does this market information actually mean for the decision in front of us?

A team leader who reads market signals accurately sets a higher standard for pricing recommendations than one who relies on intuition about which direction the market is heading. A brokerage owner who can identify which segments are absorbing fastest and where buyer pools are concentrating can make decisions about agent deployment and marketing emphasis with more precision. An association presenting market data to its members provides something more useful when the presentation explains what the indicators mean in combination and what they imply for the decisions those members are actually making.

The investors, media commentators, policy advocates, and analysts who represent a secondary audience for this book are working with the same underlying problem. A policy case for housing supply made with absorption-rate and months-supply analysis is more precise than one built from anecdote. An investment recommendation grounded in cap-rate interpretation, rent-trend analysis, and financing assumptions is more rigorous than one built from the assumption that rising prices imply rising returns. The application changes across those contexts. The professional use does not: convert common data into reasoning specific enough to guide action.

Situation	Weak Interpretation	Market-Literate Interpretation	Better Advice
Rising Inventory	"Buyers have leverage"	"Leverage is concentrated where supply is stale, substitutable, or overpriced"	Target listings with age, price reductions, or weak traffic
Rising DOM	"The market is weak"	"Longer marketing time matters when similar homes are moving faster"	Adjust price or positioning before age becomes the story
Elevated Rates	"Buyers have disappeared"	"Payment pressure has narrowed the pool of able buyers"	Solve for monthly payment: price, credits, or buydown
Increased Price Reductions	"Prices are falling"	"Sellers are resetting expectations unevenly by tier and age"	Read timing, size, and concentration before changing strategy
Nearby New Construction	"More supply is bad for sellers"	"Builder incentives change the buyer's net comparison"	Compete against the package, not just the asking price

The interpretation determines the advice. The data alone does not.

Market Literacy Takeaway

Market literacy becomes an advantage when it changes the recommendation, not just the report. The same data can support weak advice or precise advice, and the professional difference shows up in which one reaches the client.

Use This When

- You are pricing a listing and need to distinguish the metro-area trend from the segment-level conditions before giving a recommendation
- A client challenges your recommendation with a statistic from a report, a news source, or another agent
- You are explaining a negotiation posture and the basis for it needs to be specific market evidence rather than a general read of conditions
- A buyer concludes that rising inventory means equal advantage on every available listing
- A seller wants to price above the comps because the metro-area median has risen year over year

- You are presenting a market update to a team, brokerage, or client group and need to explain what the conditions mean, not just what they are
- An investor, association, media, or policy conversation requires a market explanation precise enough to withstand challenge

Be Careful When

- Repeating statistics without connecting them to a specific recommendation; data without direction is a report, not advice
- Treating market context as property-level guidance; the metro-area trend does not price the house, and the broad inventory count does not determine the offer strategy for a specific listing
- Applying broad market conditions to a specific decision without segment-level analysis of the price band, property type, and geography that actually apply
- Projecting certainty about future conditions where genuine uncertainty exists; acknowledge what is unknown and explain how the strategy accounts for it
- Letting a favorable market condition become a substitute for accurate pricing analysis; a strong market reduces the cost of a pricing error, but it does not eliminate it
- Confusing interpretive confidence with predictive ability; the goal is not to call the market correctly every time but to reason about it clearly enough that the mistakes are diagnosable and improvable

Client Explanation

What I can tell you is what the data shows in the part of the market that actually applies to your decision, and why I read it the way I do. The headline number gives us context. The analysis I do is filtered for your price range, your property type, and your timeline. When you understand why the recommendation follows from the evidence, you can make this decision knowing the reasoning behind it, not just the conclusion.

CONCLUSION

Better Interpretation, Better Decisions

The market will always produce more numbers than any professional can use. New data arrives every month: median prices, active inventory counts, days on market, absorption rates, permit totals, rate surveys, price reduction percentages. The volume does not diminish. The question is not how to collect more of it, or how to display it more attractively, or how to quote it with more confidence than the evidence actually supports. The question is which numbers matter for the decision in front of you, what they actually measure, and what should change because of them.

That question has driven every chapter in this book.

What the Book Has Argued

The argument is not against data. The chapters on median and mean, months' supply, absorption rate, the pricing path, days on market, new construction signals, and investment metrics are dense with data. The book is built on the premise that specific, accurate market information is necessary for good real estate practice.

The argument is more precise: a statistic can be correct and still be misused. A market report can be honest and still be incomplete for the question the client is asking. A figure that accurately describes the broader metro area can fail to describe the neighborhood, the price band, or the product type where the decision will actually be made. Accurate data placed in the wrong context, applied to the wrong geography, or read without accounting for seasonality and composition effects can produce advice that is defensible on its surface and wrong for the client in practice.

The seller who applies the metro-area median directly to their home's expected price is not working from false data. The metric is accurate. What is not accurate is the inference that the aggregate figure translates automatically to their specific property, in its specific condition, in its specific sub-market. The buyer who reads rising inventory as a license to negotiate on every listing is not misreading the count. What they are missing is the segmentation that would tell them where leverage is actually concentrated and where it is not.

Both are making the same structural error: using an accurate number to answer a question it was not designed to answer.

The Questions Worth Carrying Forward

This book has taught specific metrics: what each one measures, what it hides, how it connects to others, and what professional action it supports. Those specifics are the content. The framework underneath them is the part worth carrying into every market conversation you will have after putting this book down.

Before applying any market number, ask four questions:

Measure: what does this number actually count?

Context: what geography, segment, and time window produced it?

Question: what is the client actually trying to decide?

Decision: does this number change the recommendation, and how?

Those questions are deliberately simple. They are not a substitute for the chapter-level detail that came before them. They are the habit underneath it: know what the number measures, know where it came from, know what decision is being made, and know whether the number changes the advice.

Reasoning Under Uncertainty

Market literacy does not make the market certain. This is worth stating plainly because the alternative reading of any "improve your market knowledge" argument is that better analysis produces predictable outcomes, and it does not.

Mortgage rates will move in directions that are not fully visible in advance. Absorption will shift in ways that data from the prior quarter did not anticipate. Buyer behavior will respond to conditions that no market report captures in real time. The best market read in the world is still a read of the past, used to make a judgment about a future that has not yet closed.

What changes for the market-literate professional is not the certainty of the outcome. What changes is the quality of the reasoning and the visibility of the work behind the recommendation. When a pricing recommendation is grounded in segment-level evidence rather than a headline percentage, the agent can explain it, defend it under challenge, and adjust it as conditions shift without starting from scratch. When an offer strategy is grounded in a specific read of where leverage concentrates rather than a general read of the market, the client understands why that particular posture makes sense for that particular listing.

Visible reasoning is improvable. When a market read is explicit enough that both the agent and the client can engage with it, errors are diagnosable. The composition shift that moved the median was not anticipated. The seasonal compression was more pronounced than the prior year's pattern suggested. The buyer pool in that segment was more constrained by affordability than the active listing count implied. Each of those is a piece of information that refines the next read, because the framework was clear enough to reveal where the gap between expectation and result came from.

That is what separates a disciplined market read from a confident guess. A confident guess can only be defended by confidence. A disciplined read can be examined, challenged, revised, and improved.

What Better Interpretation Produces

Better interpretation does not guarantee better outcomes. It does produce better-reasoned advice, and over time that is the foundation professional credibility is built from.

In practice, better interpretation shows up in three places most directly.

Pricing decisions that are grounded in segment-level evidence. What buyers in the relevant price band, property type, and geography have been paying, how quickly well-positioned listings have been moving, and what the close-to-original-list ratio says about how the market is responding to current inventory. That analysis is what allows a pricing recommendation to hold when the client pushes back, because the evidence behind it is specific enough to discuss.

Negotiation positions that are calibrated to the particular listing's situation. Not to the general inventory count, but to where that listing falls in the spectrum between a fresh, well-priced home with active competition and a stale listing where the seller has not yet accepted what buyers have been telling the market for weeks. The distinction is available in the data. Arriving at the conversation without it means arriving without the most useful part of the analysis.

Client explanations that connect evidence to recommendation in language the client can follow, challenge, and repeat. The client who understands why the recommendation follows from the evidence can engage with it as a participant rather than accepting it as a verdict. That quality of explanation is what earns trust that survives a difficult transaction.

Market Data Is Not Market Understanding

This book opened with that claim, and it closes with the same one.

The data is available. Every agent in every market can pull a median price, a months' supply figure, an absorption rate, a close-to-list ratio, a price reduction count, a new construction completion total, a mortgage rate survey. The access is roughly equal, and in many cases so is the data itself: the same MLS, the same county reports, the same publicly available economic figures.

What is not equal is what each professional does with those numbers. Whether they connect them to the right question. Whether they segment to the sub-market where the decision actually lives. Whether they read a seasonal pattern for what it is rather than announcing a market shift. Whether they explain a contradictory signal rather than select the more convenient one. Whether they translate the analysis into advice that the client can understand, act on, and defend to the people in their lives who were not in the room.

That is what market literacy produces. Not certainty. Not prediction. Not a simpler market. A clearer way to read it.

Market data is everywhere. Market understanding is earned.

About the Author

Cooper Thayer is a Colorado-based residential real estate broker, market analyst, and industry strategist. As an actively producing agent alongside his family with The Thayer Group, he represents buyers, sellers, and investors in live residential transactions, with a focus on pricing, positioning, negotiation, and execution.

His broader work sits at the intersection of brokerage, data, market interpretation, policy, technology, and industry strategy. Cooper serves as Chief Market Strategist for the Keller Williams Realty Colorado Region and as a Market Trends Spokesperson for the Colorado Association of REALTORS®, helping agents, brokers, association leaders, legislators, and the public understand what residential real estate data actually means. The emphasis is practical, not academic or abstract.

Cooper regularly presents market analysis to brokers, legislators, and industry audiences, and his analysis has been featured in television, radio, print, and other Colorado media coverage. His work is built around making complex market information usable: not just what the numbers say, but what they imply for pricing, affordability, negotiation, consumer behavior, and professional advice. The point is practical judgment, not data for its own sake.

His particular specialty is bringing an analytical, data-driven approach to residential real estate without losing sight of the human decisions behind the numbers. Mastering Market Trends grew out of that work: the repeated gap between having access to market data and knowing how to interpret it well enough to advise a client, price a property, understand a segment, or explain what is actually happening in the market.

Cooper's goal is to help clients, professionals, and industry leaders read residential real estate more clearly, connect market information to better decisions, and bring a higher standard of reasoning to the conversations that shape the industry.

For contact info and more, visit
www.cooperthayer.com

If this book helped you explain the market more clearly, consider leaving a short review wherever you purchased it. A few honest sentences about what you found useful would mean a great deal.

Thank you.

www.ingramcontent.com/pod-product-compliance
Lightning Source LLC
LaVergne TN
LVHW021129300926
849160LV00010B/923